S0-ASI-095

Z
NB41
J021

HB

Davis

**WOMEN IN POWER IN
PARLIAMENTARY DEMOCRACIES**

U OF NEBRAS

Hardcover: 176 pages ;   45.00
Publisher: Univ of Nebraska
Pr; (March 1997)
ISBN: 0803217072
no pbk.

SJT LSYL   political
                          science

(no)
pbk

12⁵²

**Women and Power
in Parliamentary
Democracies**

Women and Politics

VOLUME 2

Series Editor

Susan Welch
Pennsylvania State University

Advisory Editors

Diane Blair
University of Arkansas

Janet K. Boles
Marquette University

Paula D. McClain
University of Virginia

Arlene W. Saxonhouse
University of Michigan

Donley T. Studlar
West Virginia University

Women and Power in Parliamentary Democracies

Cabinet Appointments in

Western Europe, 1968–1992

REBECCA HOWARD DAVIS

University of Nebraska Press, Lincoln and London

© 1997 by the University
of Nebraska Press
All rights reserved
Manufactured in the United
States of America
⊗ The paper in this book meets
the minimum requirements of
American National Standard
for Information Sciences—
Permanence of Paper for
Printed Library Materials,
ANSI Z30.48-1984. Library
of Congress Cataloging-in-
Publication Data
Davis, Rebecca Howard, 1964–
Women and power in parliamen-
tary democracies: cabinet
appointments in Western Europe,
1968–1992 / Rebecca Howard
Davis. p. cm.—(Women and
politics; v.2) Includes biblio-
graphical references and index.
ISBN 0-8032-1707-2 (cloth: alk.
paper) 1. Women in politics—
Europe. 2. Women cabinet
officers—Europe. I. Title.
II. Series: Women & politics
(Lincoln, Neb.); v. 2.
HQ1236.5.E85D38   1997
320'.082—dc20
96-22358   CIP

To my family, the source of much joy

CONTENTS

Figures

Tables

ACKNOWLEDGMENTS

This work began many years ago as a term paper in a graduate seminar. It has been reincarnated many times, as a master's thesis, a doctoral dissertation, and now a book. That I visualize this work's history as a series of births and rebirths is no doubt tied to the fact that I have had two children in the course of writing it. To many who view "the personal" and "the professional" as clearly distinct realms of an individual's life, it probably seems odd that my view of the work weaves all this history together. To me, however, Sam's and Libby's stories and the history of this work are interwoven. The birth of each of my children filled me with creative energy that has spilled over into my work and onto these pages. No doubt, I could not have gotten through the process of data collection and coding—work that I found, at times, to be sheer drudgery—had it not been for the joy I felt as I anticipated Sam's birth. Similarly, I've taken pleasure in readying this manuscript, about women and public life, for print at the time that I've given birth to a daughter.

In the course of researching and writing, I have been assisted, sustained (physically and spiritually), and encouraged by many without whom, I am certain, this work would never have been completed.

I am grateful for the financial support of the Department of Political Science and the Graduate School of Arts and Sciences at Emory University in Atlanta. The Department of Women's Studies also provided me with financial assistance to attend a planning session of the United Nations in Vienna for a proposed Conference on Women in Public Life, a conference that, disappointingly, never transpired. Although the eventual outcome of this (non-)conference was a disappointment to me as a feminist, the planning session nonetheless provided me with information and contacts that were instrumental in completing this project. Of those who also attended this planning session, I especially appreciate the assistance of Monique Leijenaar of The Netherlands and Hege Skjeie of Norway, each of whom provided information on women in her country, and Christina Pintat of the Inter-Parliamentary Union, who was very generous in sharing data gathered by the IPU on women in national parliaments.

Each member of my graduate committee—Tom Lancaster, Beth Reingold, Karen O'Connor, and Joanne Bryzynski—has made valuable suggestions. I am particularly grateful to my adviser, Tom Lancaster, who has been a mentor in the full sense of the word, and to Beth Reingold, who read all drafts carefully and was my window into the junior professorate. One of the many ways that these two earned my respect and gratitude was through the good humor, patience, and flexibility they demonstrated over the occasional participation in this project of my son, Sam. There were times with each of them that meetings included Sam. Because of Sam's age and nature, he had little interest in this research and great interest in things like exploring their offices and rearranging their books and notes (often while spilling juice or depositing trails of cracker crumbs).

As I have presented several parts of this work at conferences while the work was in progress, I also benefited from the encouragement and comments of other scholars. I am especially grateful to Donley Studlar in this respect. I owe a special debt to Donley, as he commented on an earlier version of this manuscript as well.

An earlier version of chapter 4 was presented at the 1995 annual meeting of the Western Political Science Association, as "Parliamentary Recruitment Norms and the Appointment of Women to Cabinet Positions in Western Europe, 1968–1992." Earlier versions of chapter 5 were presented at the 1994 annual meeting of the Midwest Political Science Association, as "Party Competition and the Recruitment of Women," and at the 1994 annual meeting of the American Political Science Association, as "Women and Appointments: Party Competition and the Critical Mass." An earlier version of chapter 6 was presented with Thomas Lancaster, as "The Electoral Cycle of Appointments: Timing, Incumbency, and the Appointment of Women" at the 1992 annual meeting of the American Political Science Association.

During the final semester of my work at Emory, I lived in Virginia and commuted to Atlanta along with Sam and my husband, Russell, who similarly was completing a graduate degree. We are very grateful for those friends who housed us during that semester: Bill and Jan, Janet and Ken, and Kim and Doug. We are glad to still call them friends despite having stayed long enough to have worn out our welcome.

Russell and I are also grateful to John and Helen Simmons, who allowed us to park in their driveway, saving the cost of parking permits (several hundred dollars over the years) and the uncertainty about being able to find a parking space (to say nothing of the fact that their driveway was a more secure place to leave our car than some of the alternatives—but that's another story). Anyone who thinks this was inconsequential knows nothing about the financial challenges of earning a graduate degree (degrees, in our case) or the availability of parking spaces on an urban campus.

I am also appreciative of several of my fellow graduate school sojourners. In the early stages of this project, Greg Haley and David Patterson spent many hours giving me advice and assistance with coding, entering, and analyzing data. When I realized in the final stages of preparing the manuscript that I had neglected to note some page numbers of a journal that the library of Virginia Tech does not carry, Sue Davis was generous enough to run them down for me back at Emory. Also, the friendships I have shared, especially with Dawn Nowacki, have been a source of strength.

Many other friendships have been a source of sustenance as well. I am especially grateful to Janet, whose love for Sam freed me to devote attention to work while Sam was very young, and to Kim, who remains, since seventh grade, one of my closest and dearest friends. Further, I am grateful to Kathy Jones, who allowed me to be a refugee from my domestic responsibilities at her house for a few days as I was trying to wrap this all up.

Although I mention Russell last, his support has by no means been least important. I am grateful for our partnership and for his wholly unobjective faith in my abilities.

Women and Power
in Parliamentary
Democracies

I

Introduction

Margaret Thatcher, Simone Veil, Benazir Bhutto, Corazon Aquino, Mary Robinson, Edith Cresson, and Gro Harlem Brundtland have captured a great deal of media attention. These world leaders are as noteworthy for their gender as they are for the direction they have provided to their respective political systems. Indeed, female government members, aside from the category of female government leaders, are so rare as to be almost an intellectual curiosity.

Why is this the case? Why does the female half of the world's population occupy an almost universally low fraction of the world's positions of power? What factors account for women's inroads into government in some countries while women are absent from decision-making bodies in others? Further, what difference does the descriptively unrepresentative nature of government bodies make in terms of policy outcomes? (On descriptive representation, see Pitkin 1967.)

The purpose of this study is to explain the variation across time and space in the participation of women in government in fifteen Western European parliamentary and parliamentary-type systems—those of Austria, Belgium, Denmark, Finland, France, Germany, Greece, Ireland, Italy, The Netherlands, Norway, Portugal, Spain, Sweden, and the United Kingdom.[1] The varying rates of participation of women in the formal political arena have both universal and idiosyncratic explanations (Lovenduski 1993). In recent years, scholars have begun to call for a movement away from the particular and specific (Lovenduski 1993; Norris 1993). By including fifteen countries in this study, I hope to do just that: to search for explanations that are general in nature, that account not only for the high levels of representation in Norway and Sweden but also for the low levels of representation in Italy and the United Kingdom.

The Appointment of Women

A great deal has been written in the last twenty years discussing the electoral fortunes of women (for example, Darcy, Welch, and Clark 1994; Rule 1989). Much of this literature has focused on the United States and, to a lesser extent, Great Britain. Little research has extended the focus beyond these two cases. Even less has been written about women's access to power through appointive channels.[2] Thus there are considerable gaps in the literature concerning the elite recruitment of women.

That so little has been written about the appointment process is problematic because it is often thought that minorities and women are even more disadvantaged in the process of appointment than they are in the process of election (Putnam 1976). Pippa Norris (1987) notes, for example, that the move to change the European Parliament from an appointed to an elected institution in 1979 resulted in sizable increases in the number of female European members of parliament (EMPs).

There are also two rich bodies of literature on cabinet governments. The first is what Laver and Schofield (1990) refer to as "the European Politics Tradition" (for example, Blondel and Müller-Rommel 1988; Blondel 1991). Most of this literature has focused on the evolution of cabinet systems, the preeminence of the prime minister, the nature of the ministerial career, and the recruitment of ministers to office. In general, research on cabinet systems has been framed temporally or spatially in ways that have made the number of female ministers in the studies too few to allow for cross-national generalizations or for generalizations about the differences in the recruitment of men and women. (Two notable attempts are de Winter 1991 and MacDonald 1989.)

A second well-developed tradition within the study of cabinet systems is the game theoretic approach, grounded in the work of William Riker (1962).[3] This tradition has taken up questions of government formation (which parties receive what portion of the political spoils—cabinet portfolios) and government termination.[4] This research has taken the political party almost exclusively as its unit of analysis. Thus intraparty politics are not examined.

The literature on women and politics does not address the appointive channel of recruitment and is often not comparative, while the literature on cabinet government, though often comparative and well versed on selection by appointment, does not address the selection of women. It is these gaps in the literature that this study will address. By examining every cabinet appointment in fifteen countries over twenty-four years, this study generates a sufficiently large pool of female appointments to allow for analysis of and generalizations about the ways that recruitment patterns are gendered.

Plan and Scope of the Study

The following chapter describes the participation of women in government in the fifteen countries listed previously. The original data set that has been constructed for this purpose traces the participation of women in government from 1968 to 1992. Although the selection of this time frame excludes the leadership of some noteworthy female ministers such as Nobel Peace Prize–winning Alva Myrdal, who served as the Swedish minister of disarmament in the early 1960s, women were not nominated to national executives except in small numbers before the late 1960s. Denmark is illustrative. Although a woman was appointed shortly after women won the suffrage in 1924, there were no women in the Danish government for almost fifty years afterward (Kaplan 1992; Hansen et al. 1985). In many other countries, women have been completely absent from this tier of government or their inclusion can be termed nothing other than tokenism (Lovenduski 1986). Extending the research further back in time gives little to analyze.

This study examines a period of recent history that was ushered in by an enormous political and social upheaval. In 1968, dissent flourished in the Prague Spring as well as in student movements throughout much of the Western world, most notably in France, Italy, and Germany. In 1968, the United States was engaged in Vietnam. The People's Republic of China was in the throes of the Cultural Revolution. Domestic politics in Germany, the United Kingdom, and The Netherlands were in the midst of significant transition in the late 1960s as well. In Germany, the governing Grand Coalition ended Christian Democratic hegemony. In The Netherlands, 1967 marked the end of consociational practices. Further, Richard Rose's rich and detailed study of the British cabinet system (1987) indicates that the internal structure of the cabinet was in transition during the mid to late 1960s.[5]

It was a time of change. This era spawned the so-called second wave of the feminist movement (Lovenduski 1986; Randall 1987; Kaplan 1992). As Joni Lovenduski describes the time period, "ideas about sex equality were in the air" (Lovenduski 1993, 5). These enormous political and social changes, particularly the efforts of second-wave feminists, form the backdrop for this study.

The Second Wave

The second wave of feminism refers to "certain recent clusters in women's activities on a global scale" (Kaplan 1992, 7).[6] Kaplan's (1992) work on second-wave feminism in Western Europe, unparalleled in either depth or breadth, highlights the fact that the term *second wave* is a bit of a misnomer.[7] The women's movements of the United Kingdom or the Scandinavian countries cannot, for the most part, be said to have experienced a second wave distinct from the first. Rather, they have seen more or less continuous extension of women's rights from the period termed the first wave through the era of the second wave. In contrast, the recently democratized southern European countries of Portugal, Greece, and Spain have essentially experienced a first wave of feminism during the second-wave epoch (Lovenduski 1986; Randall 1987; Kaplan 1992).

Further, some countries experienced both a first and a second wave of feminism but had the gains of the first wave—and the accumulated knowledge of those gains—eroded during periods of fascism. Such was the case in Germany, where notable socialist feminists such as Clara Zetkin and Rosa Luxemburg were international leaders of the first wave of the feminist movement (Lovenduski 1986; Kaplan 1992). In the wake of National Socialism, whose mantra was "Kinder, Küche, Kirche" (children, kitchen, church), German women of the 1960s confessed no knowledge of German first-wave feminists. Although Kaplan (1992, 108) attributes this "general amnesia" at least in part to the misogyny of the Nazi regime, it may be more a result of the interruption of regular patterns of intergenerational communication within families and schools as a result of specific historical discontinuities in the German experience (Dalton 1989).

Mussolini's fascist dictatorship did not similarly wipe out collective memory of first-wave accomplishments in Italy, largely because of the key role women played in the resistance of the *partigiani* (partisans). Indeed, the skills that Italian women developed in mobilizing during their underground days carried forward and contributed to the strength of their second-wave movement. There is more or less scholarly unanimity that the Italian second-wave movement was the strongest, best organized, and most sustained in Western Europe (Lovenduski 1986; Randall 1987; Kaplan 1992).

Of course, one of the earliest, most colorful, and most short lived of all European second-wave movements was that of the Icelandic Redstockings. At the beginning of the United Nations Year of the Woman (1975), 90 percent of all Icelandic women went on strike, leaving work—both in and out of the home—to men and effectively bringing the island to a standstill. In 1984, women in Iceland staged a well-publicized grocery store demonstration, jamming neighborhood markets and offering to pay sixty-six cents on the dollar for all goods they attempted to purchase. If women earned only sixty-six cents for every dollar men earned, they reasoned, then women should have to pay only 66 percent of the price of consumer goods. Of course, Icelandic women are probably best known for successfully transforming their social movement into a parliamentary actor, a transformation in which those on their Women's List (*Kwenna Listin*) took over the parliamentary balance of power, making them sole arbiter among contending coalitions in the process of government formation (Kaplan 1992; Thomas 1994).

The well-known exploits of Icelandic women raise the question of the exclusion of the Icelandic case from this study, as well as more general questions about the sample of parliamentary democracies represented here. Because of time constraints in construction of the data set (more fully described in the following chapter), I chose only those parliamentary democracies that were members of the European Union (EU) or the European Free Trade Association (EFTA). Although this method afforded the advantages of the area studies approach, it nevertheless precluded countries that might otherwise have logically been included, such as New Zealand, Australia, or Canada. Within the universe of EU and EFTA countries, Luxembourg and Iceland were excluded because limited information is available on these countries. Switzerland was excluded because its system of cabinet post allocation differs significantly from those of the fifteen countries included in this study. The Swiss exceptionalism in this regard is lamentable because inclusion of Switzerland would have introduced even greater variation among the disparate countries of this study, as the Swiss participatory democracy has been extreme in its resistance to extending full democratic rights to women. Swiss women were not extended the right to vote until 1972.[8] Further, the Swiss have not ratified the Social Charter of 1965 of the European Council on equal pay and working conditions. Although marriage law was belatedly amended in 1988 to treat men and women equally, Swiss women still cannot elect to maintain their maiden names in marriage (Kaplan 1992).

Although the Swiss and Icelandic variants have been excluded from this study, the country sample nonetheless has considerable variation and vibrancy. The second-wave movements of the countries examined here differed in terms of organization, tactics, longevity, and emphasis. Even among the Nordic countries in the sample, considerable differences are evident. Finnish women worked actively within the political parties of their system, whereas the Danish movement, after the women's cells were abolished in 1970 in the name of equality, operated almost entirely exogenous to the Danish political parties. The Swedish second-wave feminist movement was notable primarily for its weakness.[9] Karin Andersson, former chair of the Swedish Equality Committee, noted, "It is difficult to struggle for something on which formally everyone agrees" (as quoted in Gelb 1989, 168, and Eduards, Halsaa, and Skjeie 1985, 141). Perhaps for this reason, gender is not perceived to be a legitimate source of political conflict in Sweden. Gelb (1989, 174) terms gender conflict in Sweden "anti-Swedish." The Norwegian movement, in stark contrast, was very angry and confrontational. Norwegian women also suffered a much more significant backlash (Kaplan 1992; Bystydzienski 1988).

Although there was significant national variation among the second-wave movements of Western Europe, there were also some important commonalities. Central to many of the movements were efforts to liberalize abortion laws (Norris 1987).[10] In 1970, when the annual number of illegal abortions in The Netherlands was estimated to be ten to fifteen thousand, Dutch women disrupted a gynecological conference, displaying "Baas in eigen Buik" (boss of one's own belly) written across their midsections (Kaplan 1992, 155). Similarly, the movement's touchstone in Germany was a published "confession" by 374 well-known women that they had had abortions (Kaplan 1992). The estimated annual number of illegal abortions in Spain was three hundred thousand in 1978, when 9 women accused of having obtained abortions were put on trial in Bilbao. In a dramatic display of solidarity, two "confessions" similar to that in Germany were issued. Thousands of Spanish women signed the first one, publicly acknowledging that they had had abortions and demanding that they be tried along with the Bilbao women. In a second confession, Spanish men who had participated in abortions joined the women in demanding that they, too, be tried. Spanish men and women demonstrated and held sit-ins protesting the trial of the Bilbao women for two years, ultimately forcing the charges to be dropped (Astelarra 1992; Kaplan 1992).

Second-wave movements throughout Western Europe had many other commonalities, including the questioning of gender roles and the public/private dichotomy. The questioning of gender roles is evident in the increased support for women in political life. A longitudinal analysis of public opinion on women in national legislatures in several Western European countries found "an emerging consensus among West European men and women that women should be afforded equal participation in the political sphere. This consensus has not emerged by generational replacement; instead the attitudes of men and women of all age groups seem to have fundamentally changed" (Wilcox 1991, 144).[11]

Initially, many parts of the second-wave movement eschewed mainstream politics, believing that parties and parliaments were fundamentally hierarchical and patriarchic. Parts of the second-wave movement preferred autonomous, loosely organized, separatist organizations during the early stage of the movement. Many of the more radical elements of the movement later reconsidered the necessity of participation in mainstream politics (Lovenduski 1986, 1993; Lovenduski and Randall 1993; Kaplan 1992; Eduards et. al 1985). For example, Jill Bystydzienski (1988, 1992a) has detailed the way that the organized strands of radical (liberationist) and liberal (equal rights) feminism in Norway gradually built a coalition through which they could campaign for greater inclusion in the political process from both within and without the political mainstream.

During the second wave of the feminist movement, political parties across Western Europe came under pressure to adopt policies attractive to female voters and to provide greater opportunities for women's participation in the formal political arena, even in those countries in which a well-organized women's movement did not develop (Lovenduski 1993; Appleton and Mazur 1993; Kolinsky 1991, 1992, 1993; Galligan 1993; Guadagnini 1993; Sainsbury 1993; Leijenaar 1991, 1993; Skjeie 1993; Bystydzienski 1988; Carroll 1984; Matland 1994a, 1994b). John Major no doubt felt that pressure when a public outcry followed the announcement of his first government, which did not include a single woman (Norris and Lovenduski 1993). In a subsequent reshuffle, he was careful not to repeat his mistakes—he appointed not one, but two, women to the cabinet.

In fact, the appointment of women to government positions is one way that governments can respond to the feminist movement, relieving more general pressure for change (Carroll 1984). Appointments are highly symbolic in nature (Martin 1989). Urging his Christian Democratic Party to adopt quotas for women representatives, German Chancellor Helmut Kohl argued, "If we want to get a start into the future we have to do it now. . . . The image of the CDU is colored by how it deals with change in society" (as quoted by Miller 1994).

Although parties of the political right may now be concerned about an erosion of support by women, if there had been a gender gap in Western European politics before the 1960s (and even after that in some places), the gap was one in which women tended to give greater support than men to conservative parties (Miller 1994; Duverger 1955; Norris and Lovenduski 1993; Kolinsky 1993; Appleton and Mazur 1993; Lovenduski 1986; Jelen, Thomas, and Wilcox 1994).[12] Lovenduski and Randall (1993) argue that the changing behavior of women voters presented both incentives and pressure for parties of the left.

The pressure for inclusion of women, therefore, was probably most keenly felt by parties of the left that had not been the traditional beneficiaries of women's support. In the United Kingdom, revitalized women's sections of the Labour Party—made up of greater numbers of younger women with experience in the women's liberation movement—became increasingly militant at each party conference. In fact, some feminist campaigners within the party are described as being "taken aback" by the urgency and impatience of the younger women's pressure tactics (Lovenduski and Randall 1993, 142).

Women's demands were not the only new pressures on political parties during this era. A number of new parties emerged, most notably the German Greens, making electoral politics more competitive during this time. Further, there is considerable accumulated evidence that the electorates themselves may have changed in ways that would more directly challenge political parties (Inglehart 1977, 1990; Dalton et al. 1984; Dalton 1989).[13] One study suggests that changes in the electorate may have altered the ways that political parties operate internally, making them more responsive to grassroots demands (Rohrschneider 1994).

In the Wake of the Second Wave

The following chapter examines the extent to which women have taken advantage of the changes in the social and political system by entering and participating in government at the highest levels. In general, the law of increasing disporportions holds that women are present in lesser numbers at higher levels of government. Cabinet positions are indeed the pinnacle of power in parliamentary democracies, but there is a hierarchy within each cabinet. In most countries, women are most numerous on the bottom rungs of these hierarchies. Further, most female cabinet ministers hold portfolios concerned with a very narrow range of issue areas. Given these general trends, there are significant regional variations in women's participation in cabinet government (discussed in chapter 2).

The question of whether or not female ministers behave differently in office from male ministers is beyond the scope of this study. Nonetheless, chapter 2 discusses some of the ways women are thought to make a difference.

Chapter 3 examines the literature on elite recruitment in general and women in politics in particular, and it discusses the arguments raised to explain the virtual absence of women from the formal political arena. Many scholars interested in the participation of women in politics have noted that women's absence from the "pool of eligibles" (Darcy et al. 1994) is one of the primary factors limiting their recruitment to office. Chapter 3 discusses the backgrounds of cabinet members so as to define the ministerial pool of eligibles. It then outlines women's presence in this pool and discusses the relationship between women's eligibility for office and their presence in office.

Because women's presence in parliaments significantly defines their availability for cabinet office, chapter 4 examines such parliamentary participation and its impact on women's recruitment to cabinet office.[14] Not all cabinet systems draw from the parliamentary pool in similar fashions, and there is a wide range of norms for parliamentary tenure as a requisite for cabinet office. Chapter 4 develops a useful way to distinguish among the recruitment norms of cabinet systems. This generalist/specialist distinction is a key concept for understanding the patterns of regional variation in women's ability to obtain cabinet-level appointments, as examined in chapter 2. As Darcy et al. (1994) state, it is important to note such regional differences in women's access to office, but it is more important to understand the reasons for the regional patterns. The variation is all too often attributed simply to the residual "political culture."

Blondel (1985) describes the path to government in Western European systems as the "Parliamentary-cum-Party" route. Accordingly, chapter 5 examines the role of the political party in appointments to cabinet positions, which are occupied largely by the party elite of either governing parties or coalitions of parties (Blondel 1985, 1991; Cotta 1991; Rose 1987). Chapter 5 focuses on the role of party ideology and on the interaction among parties within a system. Over much of the last decade, scholarship on women and recruitment has argued that party ideology is a key factor in explaining whether or not women hold office. This analysis challenges that longstanding contention and suggests instead that the competitiveness of the party system or the organizational culture of the parliament—specifically, the presence or absence of a critical mass of women—is a more powerful predictor of women's success in obtaining office.[15]

Whereas earlier chapters show an indirect effect of elections on appointments, chapter 6 examines the direct effect. More specifically, chapter 6 discusses the independent impact of holding elections on the process of appointments. The strong association observed between the timing of elections and the appointment of women has important implications for democratic theory.

Although this study was undertaken to examine the recruitment of women specifically through the appointive channel and the distinctiveness of the appointment process from the elective one, connections are repeatedly found between elections and appointments. Chapter 7 more fully discusses these connections. In addition, chapter 7 elaborates the findings of earlier chapters in the form of a systems model of the process of appointment of women in cabinet positions. Further, chapter 7 outlines some directions for further research.

The findings of this study will be of interest to elite theorists, feminists, and scholars of minority politics. An understanding of the causes and consequences of the male predominance in leadership positions in government is of critical interest to students of elite behavior. Elite theorists will be interested in how formerly disenfranchised groups of people can come to share power equally with groups who have always been numerically represented in government.

Although women are not a minority population in any country, they have held only a small minority of the power. The dynamics of change in the levels of representation of women will therefore be of interest to students of minority politics.[16]

For their part, feminists will be interested in how women are politically empowered. Some feminists have argued that women's absence from the political arena raises questions of justice, questions of interest representation, and—arguing that there are unique insights from the feminine experience—questions of full utilization of societal resources (Skrede 1990). John Stuart Mill raised the last of these arguments in "The Subjection of Women": "The second benefit to be expected from giving women the free use of their faculties, by leaving them the free choice of their employments, and opening to them the same field of occupation and the same prizes and encouragements as to other human beings, would be that of doubling the mass of mental faculties available for higher service of humanity" (1970, 216).

Modeling Cabinet Appointments

Many have suggested that it is impossible to discount a degree of luck in the process of appointment (Blondel 1985; Theakston 1987). Undeniably a certain degree of luck—being at the right place at the right time—factors into individual promotions. No model of the appointment process is likely ever to explain all of the cross-national, temporal, or interparty variance. Nonetheless, there are more or less clearly defined conventions in the process of selection for cabinet positions (Blondel 1985; Rose 1971; Dogan 1989; Searing 1994). Modeling the appointment process, then, is not an unreasonable goal.

There has been little attempt to discuss the relationship of what is known about the selection of ministers to the participation rates of women. This study reflects a first attempt to connect widely disparate literatures, that on cabinet government and that on women and politics, and to outline a course of study that will lead to an understanding of changes in the participation of women in government in some countries and the absence of change in others.

The "iron law" of andrarchy (Putnam 1976) no longer accurately describes parts of the political world. Understanding the process of incorporation of women into the political process will illuminate the conditions under which, or the strategies through which, other political outgroups might secure similar access to the political elite.

An oft-cited work that discussed Norwegian women in the early 1970s lamented that women were not more eager to take part in the political process (Means 1972). Given the record number of Norwegian women in office in the 1980s, the passage of time has proven that lamentation incorrect. Clearly, in 1968 women in many parts of Western Europe were poised to enter the formal political arena in unprecedented numbers. This study seeks to describe and explain their successful entrance in some countries and their continued exclusion in others.

In politics, if you want anything said, ask a man;
if you want anything done, ask a woman.

Margaret Thatcher, quoted in Brown and O'Connor,
Hammer and Tongues

2

Participation of Women in Government

Where and to what extent have women been successful in gaining admission
to the "elite of the elite"? Which portfolios have been allocated to women?
This chapter examines the extent to which women have taken advantage of
the changes in the social and political system by participating in government
at the highest levels, as cabinet ministers. The chapter then weighs some evidence of the impact of women in government, discussing the ways that male
and female officeholders are distinct.

The Cabinet

Throughout, I refer to the political executives charged with the responsibility
of running a country as the government—sometimes called the cabinet (see
Gallagher et. al 1992). Cabinets are those bodies in parliamentary systems
made up of ministers who individually and collectively are responsible to
their national legislatures for the direction and administration of government
(Rose 1987; Blondel 1985).[1]

Cabinets are curious creations. Historically, they have emerged almost ac-
cidentally from the groups of advisers surrounding monarchs—or emperors,
as in Austria (Blondel 1988, 1991; Rose 1987; Wilson 1976; Bagehot 1967).[2]
They have grown and become more specialized, particularly since World War
II. Yet they receive barely a mention in most constitutions (Blondel 1988,
1991; Dogan 1989).[3] The Council of Ministers in The Netherlands, for example, was not formally recognized by constitutional provision until 1983. Accordingly, in one parliamentary session in 1901, the Dutch prime minister
barred discussion of cabinet procedures (Andeweg 1988b).

Perhaps the constitutional silence on cabinets has contributed to their air of
mystery. Simon James claims that a politically literate British citizen will have
heard of the cabinet but will have great difficulty in describing what a cabinet
does (1992).

In Walter Bagehot's famous elaboration of the British constitution, the cabinet is described as a parliamentary committee, one with enormous power: "A Cabinet, though it is a committee of legislature assembly, is a committee with a power which no assembly would—unless for historical accidents, and after happy experience—have been persuaded to entrust to any committee" (1961, 72). Since Bagehot's time, cabinets' powers have, if anything, increased. As government has become more centrally involved in the management of the economy during the post–World War II era, the scope of cabinet work has increased (James 1992; Blondel 1988, 1991).[4] The parliamentary decline thesis—that parliaments have lost power vis à vis executives—is well known.[5]

In parliamentary systems, the cabinet is the link between the parliament and the executive. "A Cabinet is combining committee—a *hyphen* which joins, a *buckle* which fastens, the legislative part of the state to the executive part of the state. In its origin it belongs to the one, in its functions it belongs to the other" (Bagehot 1961, 71–72; emphasis in original). Of course the extent to which the cabinet is related to the parliament varies cross-nationally. In the British system, the cabinet and prime minister are literally answerable to thousands of parliamentary questions on a biweekly basis.[6] In stark contrast, during one two-year period the Finnish prime minister did not address the Eduskunta (parliament) at all. Even in the Finnish system, though, the constitution explicitly states that the cabinet, known as the State Council, must enjoy the confidence of the parliament (Nousiainen 1988).

Cabinet posts—or portfolios—are some of the most powerful political positions in the world. Cabinet ministers, appointed by the prime minister, the chancellor, or—in the case of France—the president, are the "elite of the elite" (Dogan 1989, 2).[7] In Bagehot's words, "The cabinet, in a word, is a board of control chosen by the legislature, out of persons whom it trusts and knows, to rule the nation" (1961, 70–71).

Hierarchies within Cabinets

Ministries within cabinets are not equal (Rose 1987). Hierarchies within cabinets vary both cross-nationally and within a single country over time.[8] Harold Wilson (1976) points out that the changing priorities accorded different government departments is in part a result of old challenges giving way to new. Because it is accountable to the parliament, the cabinet must be responsive to parliamentary priorities, to "its changing moods" (Wilson 1976).

Nonetheless, there are some consistencies in cabinet systems across countries over time. Dogan (1989) conceptualizes cabinets as a system of concentric circles having the prime minister at the core, surrounded by an inner circle of four to eight of the most trusted and powerful advisers. This nerve center, or inner cabinet, usually includes the ministries of finance and foreign affairs (Rose 1987; Dogan 1989). Inner cabinets are rarely designated formally or explicitly.[9]

The next tier of the system is comprised of the rest of the senior ministers, who hold official cabinet rank and full voting privileges in cabinet meetings. On the outer rim is a larger flight of associates, usually termed either secretaries of state or junior ministers.[10]

The size of governments has grown in the post–World War II era as government responsibility for new issue areas has developed. The group of junior ministers has witnessed the most growth (Blondel 1988). In some cases, growth in their numbers has occurred because it met less parliamentary resistance than did expansion in the ranks of senior ministers. In Spain, for example, where the number of senior ministers is legally mandated, any increase in the number of senior portfolios requires passage of legislation. Increasing the number of junior portfolios, however, requires no more than a government decision to do so (Bar 1988).

Cabinets vary in the degree to which they function in hierarchical or egalitarian fashion. One factor contributing to the degree to which ministers work as teams of equals is whether the government is a coalition. Single-party governments tend to be more hierarchical than coalitions (Müller-Rommel 1988). British government, characterized almost exclusively as a single-party government, is one of the most oligarchical of the cabinet systems discussed in this study. It is the British case that gave rise to much of the debate about whether or not cabinet government has become prime ministerial. The Finnish system, in contrast, is one of the most egalitarian. In the Finnish cabinet, or college of ministers, the prime minister has little power or influence beyond that of an ordinary minister. Even in the Finnish case, though, the coalition partners recognize the priority of certain issue areas by allocating two ministers to some departments and only one to others (Nousiainen 1988).

Where do women fit into these hierarchies? How do they participate in the cabinet systems of the countries of this study?

Data on Women in Government

To assess the participation of women in government in the fifteen countries of this study, information was compiled on every government change in the countries between 1968 and 1992, as reported in *Keesing's Contemporary Archives*.[11] In all, more than three hundred variables were coded for each of 5,965 cabinet-level appointments, spanning the tenure of 94 prime ministers.

The data set represents 454 cabinet reorganizations, 176 of them entailing the formation of new governments (Lijphart 1984). The remaining 278 are midterm reshuffles. The variables in this data set include measures of the par-

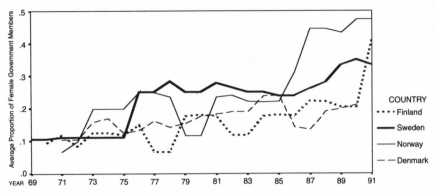

Figure 1. Women in Government: Scandinavia

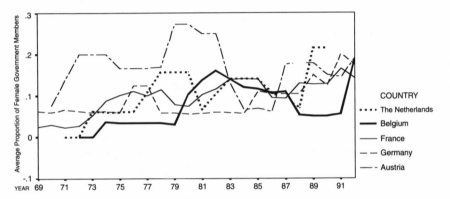

Figure 2. Women in Government: The Continent

ticipation of women in government as well as the number of parties in government, coalition type (minority or surplus majority, for example), the ideological complexion of government, and the nature of portfolios held by women
(see appendix 1 for a more complete description of the data).

It is clear that there has been change over time in the representation of
women in Western European governments (fig.1–4). Women enjoyed a
greater share of representation in 1992 than they did in 1968 in all of the
countries in this study except Portugal.

The increase in representation of women over time has not been unidirectional, nor has the same extent of change occurred in all regions of Western
Europe (fig.5). In 1992 the representation of women approached parity with
the representation of men in the Nordic countries of Norway, Finland, and
Sweden but not in Denmark. In continental Europe (Austria, Belgium, Germany, France, and The Netherlands), the representation of women ranged

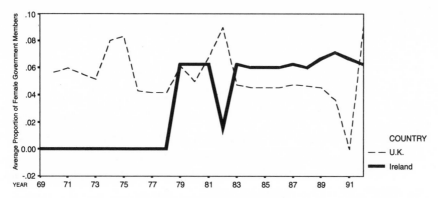

Figure 3. Women in Government: Anglo-Irish Isles

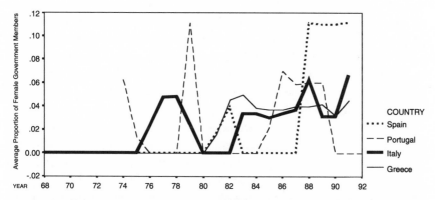

Figure 4. Women in Government: Southern Europe

between 10 and 20 percent in 1992. The 1992 levels of representation in Ireland, the United Kingdom, and Spain were between 5 and 10 percent. In the rest of the southern European countries at that time, representation levels remained at or below 5 percent.

These regional patterns suggest political culture as an explanation for the inclusion of women in government. But the sharp upward and downward movements in the trend lines of the individual countries also suggest that the fate of women has been tied to the fortunes of specific political actors. (The effect of political culture on the representation of women is examined in chapters 3 and 4.)

The absolute number of women in any of the cabinets studied ranged from zero to nine (with nine in the Brundtland cabinets of the early 1990s in Norway), while the absolute number of portfolios held by women in any of these cabinets ranged from zero to twelve (with twelve occurring in the 1978 Chris-

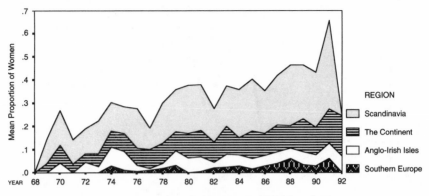

Figure 5. Women in Government by European Region, 1968–1992

tian Democratic Appeal–Liberal alliance in The Netherlands under Van Agt; in Norway under Brundtland; and following a reshuffle in the Mauroy cabinet in March of 1983 in France).[12] The fact that the number of portfolios held by women is greater than the number of women in the cabinets is a reflection of the trend for cabinet members to hold more than one functional responsibility (Blondel and Müller-Rommel 1988).

The data also reflect a strong degree of sectorization or concentration in the participation of women in government.[13] The portfolios allocated to women reflect the educational and occupational categories into which women have traditionally been channeled for work and study (table 1). Roughly 50 percent of the 438 appointments that were made to women were in the categories of health, social welfare, education, family, culture, or consumer affairs. These portfolios are not, in general, part of the inner cabinets of cabinet systems (Blondel 1988). Although many have lamented the sectorization of women in government, Lovenduski points out that "if a preponderance of women in cultural, social, or women's departments or ministries is not ideal, it is a major advance on a preponderance of men in such posts. And whilst they may be faulted for not being identifiable paths to premierships, such posts are nonetheless concerned with important subjects. It is only measurement based solely upon criteria of political clout which renders them 'unimportant'" (1986, 241).

Portfolios that were common to many of the cabinets in Western Europe and that women never held during 1968–92 include economic affairs, defense (although a woman was once appointed a junior minister of defense), relations with parliament, employment, equipment, and budget. Women have held office in only half the functional areas in which there are cabinet-level positions.

Table 1. Patterns of Sectorization of Women in Cabinet Appointments

Portfolio	Number of Times Woman Appointed	Percentage of Appointments
Social Welfare	46	12.4
Health	45	12.1
Family-youth	38	10.3
Education	38	10.3
Economic[a]	29	7.8
Culture	28	7.5
Environment	16	4.3
Development	13	3.5
Labor	13	3.5
Justice	12	3.2
Government Administration	11	3.0
Consumer Affairs	11	3.0
Ecclesiastical Affairs	11	3.0
Status of Women	10	2.7
International Affairs	10	2.7
No portfolio	9	2.4
Other	9	2.4
Leisure-sports	8	2.2
Communications	6	1.6
Prime Minister	5	1.3
Defense	3	0.8
	$N = 371$	100.00

[a]Economic portfolios such as agriculture, fisheries, shipping, foreign trade, tourism, budget, or commerce. Note that these portfolios are not the same thing as the economy, finance, or treasury portfolios, which are the highest economic portfolios.

A Link to Parliamentary Roles?

The sectorization of women in government may be the result of female concentration in parliament (such as on parliamentary committees) or of specialization outside the formal political arena. Unfortunately, there are no systematic cross-national data on parliamentary committee participation, partly because no two parliaments have identical committee systems. Further complicating the matter, committee titles do not necessarily give clear indication of substantive purview.

Data collected by the Inter-Parliamentary Union (IPU) show that at least one woman was present on every parliamentary committee in several of the countries in this study—Austria, Denmark, Germany, The Netherlands, Norway, Spain, and Sweden. Nonetheless, their data also highlight the fact that it is in the areas of family, social affairs, health, and education that women are most numerous (IPU 1992). One issue area outside the realm of women's traditional expertise and interest is defense. Extent of parliamentary defense committee participation, then, would offer a meaningful indicator of the extent to which women have moved out of the parliamentary pink ghettos. We are thus fortunate to have data on defense committee participation for several

Table 2. Parliamentary Committee Participation of European Women, 1991

Country	Defense	Health	Education	Found on all committees?
Austria	·	·	·	Yes
Belgium	4.3	·	·	·
Denmark	12.0	·	53.0	Yes
France	1.4	·	·	No
Germany	16.0	·	23.0	Yes
Greece	4.0	·	·	No
Italy	0.0	·	·	No
Netherlands	12.0	56.0	30.0	Yes
Norway	18.2	·	·	Yes
Portugal	0.0	·	·	No
Spain	0.003	·	·	Yes
Sweden	35.0	59.0	·	Yes
U.K.	0.0	·	·	No

Note: In bicameral parliaments, figures are for the lower chamber only. Participation is in percentage of committee membership. All data on committee participation are from a survey conducted by Inter-Parliamentary Union in October 1991 (IPU 1992). The survey was an ambitious undertaking designed to give a comprehensive picture of the participation of women in parliamentary institutions. In all, 146 parliaments responded to their survey, including all 15 of the countries in this study. Much of the information was inconsistently reported, however, making comparison difficult.

· = data not available.

of the fifteen countries studied. Table 2 compares the participation of women in defense committees and in health and education committees in these countries. Only in Sweden has the extent of participation of women in defense committees approached the extent of their representation in the parliament as a whole. In all the other countries, female entrants have continued to be channeled into committees dealing with health and welfare issues, even though the number of women in parliament has grown over time.

One implication of the specialization of women in Western European parliaments is that women are less visible in parliamentary arenas in general (Skard and Haavio-Mannila 1985a; Dahlerup and Haavio-Mannila 1985; Leijenaar 1991; Willis 1991). Skard (1985) argues that the issue areas in which women tend to specialize absorb less of a parliament's energy. She further argues that less debate time is consumed by these matters, making female participation in parliamentary debate less common (Skard 1985).

Although no definitive reason for the persistence of sectorization in these systems can be given, organization theory offers a few possible explanations. The first and most obvious is that women in parliaments may simply choose to specialize in areas of traditional interest. This explanation seems credible in light of related research (discussed later), which suggests that female officeholders, accord women's traditional interests greater priority. There are other possible explanations, though. Kanter (1977) suggests that majority cultures in institutional settings channel minority members into stereotypical

roles so as to accommodate their presence while maintaining their preju-
dices.[14] When Thatcher was brought into the Macmillan government, there
were two openings in the cabinet: one in aviation and one in pensions. She
writes that she couldn't imagine the position in aviation being given at that
time to a women. She therefore concluded that if she were to be invited to join
the cabinet, she would be offered—as she was—the pensions ministry
(Thatcher 1995, 117).

A final argument offered to explain the concentration of women within legislatures challenges the assumption that female parliamentarians will ever
come to resemble their male counterparts. In fact, as greater numbers of
women are elected, female parliamentarians may begin to resemble male parliamentarians even less.[15] Conformity pressures are greatest in institutional
settings in which the majority culture is clearly predominant. The freedom to
differentiate comes with the removal of token status. By this logic, as the representation of women in legislatures grows, female parliamentarians may be
more free to pursue a distinctive agenda (Thomas 1994; Flammang 1985;
Kanter 1975; Saint-Germain 1989).

In describing the relationship of women's participation in government in
Great Britain to their parliamentary participation, Lovenduski (1986) notes
that women's range of committee areas is broader than suggested by the range
of cabinet portfolios they have held. Similarly, she argues that, despite having
a limited presence in the committee system of the Italian Chamber of Deputies
(reflecting the small number of female Italian deputies), women are nonetheless well dispersed throughout the committee system (Lovenduski 1986).

At the Pinnacle of Power

Of the ninety-four prime ministers who served in Western Europe during
1968–92, four were women: Margaret Thatcher, Gro Harlem Brundtland,
Edith Cresson, and Dr. Maria de Lurdes Pintasilgo. Female prime ministers
headed the cabinets during 7 percent ($N = 32$) of all government formations
or reshuffles during this time period.[16]

Given that women have headed a sizable number of cabinets in Western Europe (although still a rare phenomenon), a natural question is whether the sex
of a prime minister affects the likelihood that other women will come to
power or be appointed to office. Some female executives have made it a point
to advance the careers of other women.[17] Gro Harlem Brundtland, for one, is
known for her commitment to promoting women and advancing women's interests. My data show a positive and statistically significant correlation ($r =$
.1411) between the proportion of women in government and the sex of the
prime minister.[18] Female prime ministers are slightly more likely than their
male counterparts to have women in their cabinets. The correlation, however,
does not necessarily imply causation.

During much of Thatcher's lengthy tenure as prime minister of the United Kingdom, she was the only women serving in her cabinet. There is no a priori reason to believe that a woman is more likely to appoint other women. In fact, there are many reasons to believe that women such as Thatcher, who have made it to the apex of political power in a system that includes few other women, will take the opposite tack—distancing themselves from other women. "When a woman is let in by the men who control the political elite it usually is precisely because that woman has learned the lessons of masculinized political behavior well enough not to threaten male political privilege" (Enloe 1989, 6–7). This statement of course raises Putnam's "so what" question: of what significance are differences in elite backgrounds (Putnam 1976)? What difference does it make whether there are greater numbers of women in government?[19]

Women in Power: What Difference Does Difference Make?

Many political commentators have suggested that female officeholders are no different from male officeholders. Observers have suggested that the few women who have made it into the highest echelons of political office are "honorary men," "surrogate men," or "exceptional women" (Lovenduski 1986; Gelb 1989). One Texan constituent probably expressed these sentiments most colorfully in referring to former governor Ann Richards, who, he mused, was simply "Bubba in drag" (Witt, Paget, and Matthews 1994, 265).

At the outbreak of the Indo-Pakistan war in 1965, controversial Indira Gandhi earned "praise" as "the only man in a cabinet of old women" (Bumiller 1990, 159). Then serving as minister of information and broadcasting, she had been vacationing in Kashmir when Pakistan invaded. Her refusal to leave the state of Kashmir until the situation stabilized was a great booster of morale for the Indian people. It is said that womanhood was irrelevant to the political life of Gandhi, who has often been characterized as ruthless and brutal. Bumiller writes that Gandhi, like Thatcher and Golda Meir, "transcended sexual categories, becoming, in the popular imagination, not man, not woman, but leader" (1990, 148).[20]

While education minister in Britain, "Maggy Thatcher the Milk Snatcher" spearheaded the repeal of government subsidies for schoolchildren's milk. In her one breach of party discipline during her tenure in the Commons, Thatcher, along with sixty-nine other Conservative party renegades, attempted to introduce caning for juvenile offenders (Thatcher 1995, 116). Her policies, then, could hardly be described as "kinder and gentler," to borrow a phrase from a recent American president. Nor was her political style softer or less confrontational. Thatcher was known for her take-it-or-leave-it management of cabinet affairs, and her intolerance of dissent was undoubtedly a factor in her ultimate political demise (Burch 1988; Marshall 1989).

Many women in positions of power—such as Thatcher, Gandhi, and Richards—are often criticized, then, for not being concerned with advancing women's rights or for adopting masculine leadership styles. Women in appointive offices often draw fire because of the potentially symbolic nature of the appointive process, as when Giscard d'Estaing appointed Françoise Giroud to the newly created position of secretary of state for the condition of women. Although arguably the best-known female journalist in France at the time, the conservative Giroud had limited connections to the women's movement. French feminists argued that the creation of the post and her appointment were largely a "public relations exercise" rather than a sincere effort to address the concerns of women (Kaplan 1992, 170). Indeed, Giroud's position was subsequently downgraded and then eliminated.

Anyone who argues that women do not make a difference in office, though, is confronted with the empirical reality that people—men and women alike—want more women in office. Dianne Feinstein's "Two Percent Is Not Enough" campaign slogan in the 1992 U.S. Senate race in California resonated with many in the wake of the Clarence Thomas confirmation hearings. When women were absent from the new coalition announced in Greece in November 1989, a storm of protest broke out. The outrage that was expressed was not limited to feminist circles but extended to the media, to the ranks of the party elite, and throughout the general public (Kaplan 1992, 227). Why would the citizenry of the United States and Western Europe want women to be present in political office if there is, in fact, no difference in substance or style between male and female representatives?

One answer is that, for every story of a Margaret Thatcher or Indira Gandhi who seems no different from the long line of men who have served in political office, there is at least one story of a female officeholder whose policies have made a difference, who has had a different style or perspective, and who has advanced otherwise neglected causes related to women. For example, Maria de Lurdes Pintasilgo, later Portuguese prime minister, in 1973 founded the first commission for social policy for women. This commission was the predecessor of Portugal's current Commission for Women's Condition, attached to the prime minister's office. Elsewhere, when the Dutch government failed to follow up on a 1989 report showing that female prostitutes did not avail themselves of social and medical services despite the high incidence of rape and assault, Ter Veld, a female junior minister, initiated parliamentary efforts to overhaul government assistance to prostitutes (Kaplan 1992).

There is growing evidence that validates what the citizenry intuits, namely, that—for whatever reasons, cultural, economic, or otherwise—women are distinct from men as officeholders. Research on legislative arenas in advanced industrial democracies has revealed differences between male and female legislators in three categories: background, role perception, and performance. An understanding of the ways that men and women as officeholders are different is imperative for a discussion of executive recruitment (chapter 3).

Background

Research in the 1970s and early 1980s found differences in family background, educational attainment, average age, and route to office among male and female legislators. The women were less likely than male legislators to be married, to enter politics without spousal support, or to have children (Carroll 1989: Burrell 1994; Hills 1983). In those cases when female legislators did have children, the children tended to be older than the offspring of male counterparts (Diamond 1977; Carroll 1989; Cantor and Bernay 1992).[21]

During this time, it was widely believed that marriage provided benefits to male, but not to female, politicians. In her autobiography, Margaret Thatcher writes, "When Denis asked me to be his wife, I thought long and hard about it. I had so much set my heart on politics that I really hadn't figured marriage in my plans" (Thatcher 1995, 67).

The prevalence throughout advanced industrial democracies of an unequal distribution of domestic responsibilities has meant that political careers for women, much like careers in other professions, have often entailed an either/or choice. For this reason, one common finding in the early research on female legislators was that they tended to enter politics later than their male counterparts (Thomas 1994; Bernstein 1986; Burrell 1994; Carroll 1989; Hills 1983; Randall 1987).

In an analysis of the personal backgrounds of political appointees in the United States, Carroll (1989) points out that women may have been more likely to defer political involvement because of their family obligations but it is also possible that those who made appointments gave less consideration to women with small children because of the perception that they were unavailable during their children's early years.

Margaret Thatcher's description of her attempts to combine political career with family responsibilities lends credibility to Carroll's speculation that party leaders may be wary of women with young children. Thatcher writes that the party's vice chairman for candidates explained "in the kindest possible way" both the difficulties of combining membership in the House of Commons with family obligations and the problems in persuading a "safe seat" to adopt her despite her family obligations (Thatcher 1995, 79). Indeed, the first several times that Thatcher appeared before district candidacy selection meetings, she was turned away after a barrage of questions about her ability to combine parliamentary representation with her roles as wife and mother.[22]

Kolinsky's (1991) examination of the backgrounds of female parliamentarians in the Bundestag (the lower house of the German parliament) in the late 1980s, although it does not offer comparisons with male legislators, found several significant differences in backgrounds among the women of different *Fraktionen*.[23] For example, she found that both Christian Democratic and Free Democratic women tended to have larger families than those who were Social Democratics, who likewise tended to have larger families than the female Greens.

In addition to the differences noted in personal backgrounds, male and female legislators have been found to differ slightly in educational and occupational status (Diamond 1977; Thomas 1994; Carroll 1984; Burrell 1994). In education, for example, although women were just as likely as men to hold a college degree, they were somewhat less likely to have obtained a graduate degree (Diamond 1977; Thomas 1994). Among political appointees at the state level, however, one study revealed that women were more likely to hold graduate degrees (Carroll 1984).

In an analysis of the German parliament, Kolinsky found that Christian Democratic women were the least likely to have a university degree, Greens women the most likely, and Social Democratic women were between the two. Kolinsky concludes, "Different party cultures attract different types of women" (1991, 66).

Perhaps because of the differences in background between male and female legislators, routes to office were often different. Many researchers found that female legislators were more likely than men to have entered politics through volunteer work or local-level politics, and women who entered through party work tended to have given more years of service (Thomas 1994; Carroll 1984; Burrell 1994). Women's "biological association" with the feminist movement may have made women more politically suspect, requiring additional years of party service and loyalty prior to recruitment (Carroll 1984).

More recent examinations of the backgrounds of male and female legislators have found that gender differences in educational attainment have narrowed over time and that female legislators are increasingly drawn from a more diverse set of occupational backgrounds (Thomas 1994; Burrell 1994).

Role Perception

The role perceptions of female representatives in the United States seem to differ greatly from those of their male counterparts in some ways but are quite similar in others. Female delegates have been found to value the aspects of their jobs that stress civic duty, while men have been more inclined to highlight legislative effectiveness or status within the legislative chamber (Thomas 1994; Cantor and Bernay 1992). These views may reflect different understandings of the appropriate use of power (Cantor and Bernay 1992).

Although women are just as likely as men to see themselves as delegates or trustees, women are more likely to see themselves as representatives of other women (Reingold 1991; Thomas 1994). Women are more likely to give priority to legislation about women, and they are more likely to take pride in legislative accomplishments in areas of traditional concern for women—that is, legislation concerning women, children, families, education, and medical and welfare issues (Thomas 1994). No matter what the issue, "foreign aid, the budget, or the environment, women are more likely than men to consider the possible impact of the policy on the lives of women and children" (Carroll 1990, 11). These differences appear to hold for both liberal and conservative—feminist and nonfeminist—women (Dodson 1989; Thomas 1994; Rapoport et. al 1990).

Perhaps because women are more likely to see themselves as representatives of other women, they are more likely to sponsor legislation about women (Thomas 1994; Willis 1991; Skard 1980). Skard (1980) has shown that from 1960 to 1975, the proportion of issues discussed by Norway's Storting (parliament) related to the legal, economic, and social position of women increased from 5 percent to 25 percent. In this period, the representation of women almost doubled, from 8.6 percent of the seats in parliament after the 1961 election to 15.5 percent in the 1973 election (IPU 1991). Skard further demonstrates that female parliamentarians initiated discussion of these issues 90 percent of the time.

Performance

Much of the research on female legislators suggests that they take their role very seriously—often working harder than their male counterparts—but that they do not necessarily consider themselves more effective than men in legislative chambers. Female legislators are more likely than male legislators to attend party meetings and conferences, and they tend to work longer hours than their male counterparts (Thomas 1994; Reingold 1991). The difference in perceptions of effort and efficacy may be a result of women's status as political newcomers. Being outside the socializing networks of legislative institutions, women must work longer hours for equal measures of productivity (Thomas 1994). Yet another interpretation is that women are attempting to compensate for lesser degrees of social capital (Kanter 1977). Alternately, self-reported behavior (numbers of hours worked, for example) may differ from objective observations (Reingold 1991).

Although women have felt less efficacious in some ways, they are more productive in others. One study finds that women are more successful than men at achieving passage of bills concerned with the lives of women. The study also finds that women's greater success at enacting such legislation is not a result of the fact that they tend to give this type of legislation higher priority (Thomas 1994).

One consistent finding in the research on women as officeholders is the absence of male/female differences in voting behavior within parliaments. Female MPs are not more likely than male MPs to brook party discipline in divisions (Gelb 1989; Lovenduski 1993; Willis 1991). From voting records, then, women in parliaments do not appear to have an independent policy agenda. However, American feminist leader and political scientist Eleanor Smeal has cautioned against using voting records as an indicator of gender differences. She argues that voting records do not indicate strength of support (Smeal 1984).[24] Her caution is perhaps even more appropriately taken in reference to European politics where an individual MP faces more extreme costs for parliamentary dissent.

Because party discipline is much stricter in Western Europe than in the United States, it is appropriate to expect that if there are gendered patterns of differences in style or agenda, such differences might be manifest in cross-party dialogue or consensus building or in intraparty politics. Many have credited women MPs with influencing the direction of party policy. For example, some claim there would be no national day-care policy in Sweden if not for the Social Democratic Women's Federation (Gelb 1989).

Further evidence of the impact or potential impact of women within parties comes from the United Kingdom. When interviewed, female candidates there expressed somewhat more liberal views than men running for similar positions. Further, the women interviewed gave higher priority to issues of health, education, and nuclear energy (Norris and Lovenduski 1989). These findings suggest that greater participation of women within parties may change the nature of policy agendas.

Similarly, on the basis of sex, women have been able to bridge intraparty divisions. In the Finish Communist Party, riven through much of its history by a pro-Soviet versus Euro-Communist split, women in both camps were able to cooperate on gender-related issues (Kaplan 1992).

Further, efforts at cross-party dialogue by women on behalf of women have frequently been noted (Willis 1991; Sawer 1984; Gelb 1989; Kaplan 1992; Vallance 1979). In Sweden, for example, women of all political persuasions in the Riksdag (parliament) banded together in 1979 to demand greater representation for women. Subsequently, Swedish women have continued to discuss issues across party lines and have pressed their respective parties on such matters as cliterodectomy among immigrant women (Gelb 1989).

In Australia, a parliamentary system outside this study but having comparably high party discipline, female politicians collectively have worked for programs such as community-based funding of day care and women's education. Largely as a result of women's efforts, a woman's budget program was established in 1984, requiring the commonwealth to provide gendered analysis of its programs (Sawer 1990; Darcy, Welch, and Clark 1994).

It appears, then, that women in Western European parliaments are working within the strictures of party discipline to ensure consideration of women's lives (Matland 1994a). It appears that they are also working across party lines to the extent permissible by party discipline. In time, female officeholders may have an even greater policy impact. Many studies have found that one critical factor in women's impact on policy is the size of their presence within the legislature. As their numbers there increase, they are more effective at altering legislative content (Thomas 1994; Saint-Germain 1989).

Where women are present in only small numbers, their policy impact is negligible (Thomas 1994; Saint-Germain 1989). Isolated women in political office face a number of dilemmas or choices not similarly encountered by their male counterparts. First of all is the need to fit in and not to appear different from their male counterparts, while at the same time demonstrating that their presence makes a difference (Bystydzienski 1992a; Lovenduski 1986). They must also balance any desire to advance women's interests against desire to participate in channels of upward recruitment, since the latter means not being associated exclusively with "women's issues" (Carroll 1994; Lovenduski 1986; Gelb 1989). Still another challenge is the need to adopt to the male folkways of politics, being willing, for example, to play hardball while not appearing overly masculine.[25] As the size of women's presence in legislatures increases, these problems may diminish. Over time, those women who are present may be better able to draw attention to the impact of policy on women.[26]

Interestingly, in those arenas in which women have a sizable presence, male legislators are also more likely to sponsor legislation concerning the social, legal, and economic position of women than are male legislators in arenas in which women do not have a significant numeric presence (Thomas 1994). What are the reasons for this? Perhaps the physical presence of women raises awareness of issues concerning the lives of women. Perhaps, in legislative arenas where more women are present, male and female politicians engage in dialogue that heightens awareness among male politicians of the realities of women's lives. The dynamics of electoral competition may play a role, leading male politicians to sponsor more legislation concerning women out of concern that female politicians might steal their thunder on these issues. Alternately, the changed behavior of male politicians may be a function of the societal changes that have enabled women to be present in the legislature in the first place.

There are other reasons to expect an even greater policy impact from women's participation in legislative arenas in the future. Largely as a result of the second wave of the feminist movement, many have come to question the evaluation of traditionally masculine values and attributes as superior and the traditionally feminine as inferior. As a result, women both in and out of politics have been less reluctant to embrace gender differences in recent years. In the United States, this has manifested itself in bold and assertive campaign rhetoric by women candidates in recent elections. Commenting on the electoral fortunes of women candidates in the United States, Senator Barbara Mikulski states, "Women are finally learning that [their] private values are good enough to be public ones" (Witt, Paget, and Matthews 1994, 277).[27]

Just as women in the United States have been less reluctant to call attention to gender differences, so, too, have women in Western Europe. Bringing traditional female values into the political realm was a common justification offered in the 1980s for the inclusion of women in politics in Norway (Bystydzienski 1992).

Changes in the international arena may also affect women's effectiveness. The end of the cold war, for example, has altered the political landscape by diminishing the concern about defense and security issues and heightening the interest in domestic politics, in which women have historically been perceived as more competent.

Even if not all female officeholders are interested in addressing gender issues, their presence may nonetheless be important. Ruth Mandel of the Center for the American Woman and Politics argues that women holding political office serve as examples, encouraging and paving the way for future women (1988; see also Carroll 1994). Indeed, even Indira Gandhi, who was "typical of nothing," expanded the awareness of possibilities for Indian women (Bumiller 1990, 149).

Conclusion

Many feminists may applaud the evidence suggesting that female legislators are more likely to consider women's lives in the formation of policy. Feminists may see in this evidence justification for demands for greater inclusion, along with the hope that as more women are seated in legislatures their interests may be better represented.

The long view of history makes clear, however, that gender differences are at best a double-edged sword. In the process of government recruitment, many such differences arguably play a role in limiting women's participation in cabinet offices. Concentrating or specializing within parliaments, for example, on a set of issues that are traditionally accorded less parliamentary time and prestige may contribute to women's invisibility within legislatures. Being visible, having one's efforts and talents noted by the party leadership, plays a critical role in being tapped for government membership.

In chapter 4 I more fully discuss the norms among cabinet systems in choosing MPs for promotion. I examine in chapter 4 the extent to which parliamentary concentration inhibits women's recruitment. Women's sectorization within parliaments is more significant, I argue, in some types of cabinet systems than in others.

Norwegian feminist Birgit Brock-Utne has repeatedly said, "We don't want a piece of the pie; we want to change the basic recipe of the pie" (Bystydzienski 1992a, 14). There is some evidence that the exceptional numbers of women participating in the cabinets of Gro Harlem Brundtland have done just that.[28] Although at one time it would have been unusual for a minister to ask to be excused from a cabinet meeting to attend to family responsibilities, it is now reportedly a common occurrence for both male and female ministers to excuse themselves in order to pick up a child from day care (Bystydzienski 1992a). The participation of women in government has altered public awareness of how the personal and the political overlap.

Women who have held office have clearly had an impact on the political process. However, despite women's substantial gains in government participation over the last twenty-five years, they remain a small minority in the highest of political positions. Only in the Nordic area have women begun to be present in government positions in numbers comparable to those of men.

Further, women have held ministries outside the realm of women's traditional interests, but there remain a significant number of ministries to which women have never been appointed. Moreover, women's governmental participation continues to be concentrated heavily in the health and social welfare areas and thus conforms to the "law of increasing disproportions" (Putnam 1976; Studlar and Matland 1994). Or, as Elizabeth Vallance (1979) so aptly puts it, "Where power is, women aren't."

Under Dogan's (1989) conception of government as a system of concentric circles, women are more likely to appear in the outer ring, less likely to appear in the second tier, and least likely to be present at the core. Why have so few women reached the apex of political power? Why does women's absence from political power remain the norm in most countries, and what factors result in the anomaly of female leadership in others? The following chapter reviews the explanations suggested in the past for the poor representation of women among governing elites.

One thing we learned from the political
women we interviewed is that leadership is
learned and develops over time. We learned
that leaders do not spring forth like Athena,
fully grown from Zeus's head.

Dorothy W. Cantor and Toni Bernay,

Women in Power: The Secrets of Leadership

3

The Pool of Eligibles

Neither Thatcher nor Brundtland emerged overnight as her party's leader. Prior to being chosen leader of the Norwegian Labor Party (PvdA), Brundtland chaired the foreign affairs committee in the Storting, served on the finance committee, and worked as the party's deputy prime minister. In the Norwegian government, she held the environmental portfolio (the first in Western Europe) before the premiership. Similarly, Thatcher became party leader only after serving in several government ministries—transport, education, and pensions.

For each of them, the association with her party began long before parliamentary service. Brundtland was a member of the Labor Party's Youth Movement from the age of seven; Thatcher joined the Oxford University Conservative Association almost immediately after entering university (Thatcher 1995). Neither of these women, then, sprang forth like Athena. Each became prime minister only after developing the requisite credentials of office.

What are the credentials for ministerial office? To what extent do Western European women qualify? Is it possible that women are absent from the ranks of the political elite because they lack the requisite qualifications? Many have suggested that there are limited numbers of women in government because there are few in the "pool of eligibles" (Darcy, Welch, and Clark 1994). *New York Times* columnist Anna Quindlen refers to this argument as the "pipeline problem": the scarcity of women at the apex of power in business and the professions because of insufficient numbers coming up through the "pipelines" (Quindlen 1993, 262).

For the most part, there are no formal requirements for seeking cabinet appointment. There are, nonetheless, informal requirements for being certified as eligible for elite membership by the "gatekeepers." Those who have the proper credentials are said to belong to the pool of eligibles.

There are many notions of what constitutes the political elite. Following the example in Robert Putnam's (1976) comprehensive literature review, I define the term *political elite* broadly in terms of the distribution of power: the political elite have more of it than others. *Power* refers to the ability to influence collective decision making, that is, "the probability of influencing the policies and activities of the state, or (in the language of systems theory) the probability of influencing the authoritative allocation of value" (Putnam 1976, 6).

Although there is no unified "elite theory" of recruitment, a number of scholars have articulated generalizations about the behavior and composition of elites that collectively describe the developing body of elite theory. The first such generalization is the "iron law of oligarchy" (Mosca 1939; Michels 1959; Ranney 1965; Pareto 1966). This law holds that those who govern are a self-perpetuating, highly exclusive elite drawn disproportionately from the well-educated upper class. The law emphasizes the cohesive—almost conspiratorial—linkages among individual members of the ruling elite. In fact, however, there is considerable difference among the cabinet systems in this study in terms of the rate of elite turnover and circulation. Finland and France, for example, have very high rates of elite turnover, whereas Austria's rate is much lower (Blondel 1991; Frognier 1991). We might expect to find that countries with higher rates of elite turnover are relatively open and more easily penetrated by out-groups.

In addition to Michels's iron law of oligarchy, others have postulated that two additional laws govern the composition of elites: the "law of increasing disproportion" and the "iron law of andrarchy" (Putnam 1976). According to the first, the higher echelons of governing elites tend to be even less representative of the population as a whole than are the lower strata. The second refers to the universal tendency for women to comprise, statistically, the most underrepresented group.

Across time and space, there have been so few women in office that some have said the female half of the population is essentially disqualified from membership in the political elite from the outset (Aberbach et al. 1981, 80). Writing in 1994 about the roles of parliamentarians in the House of Commons, Donald Searing describes the "Parliament *Man*," the "Club *Man*," and the "Good House of Commons *Men*" (Searing 1994, emphasis added). Government participation is without doubt gendered. But as discussed in chapter 2, women have made inroads into government ministries in sizable numbers in some political systems. A lawlike description of elite membership thus seems less applicable today than in the past.

What are the other qualifications for membership in the political elite? What characteristics do gatekeepers require, and who are the gatekeepers to ministerial office? First of all, the political elite are disproportionately well ed-

Table 3. Women Enrolled in University Programs, 1950 and 1985

Country	Total Students		Female Students		Percentage Female	
	1950	1985	1950	1985	1950	1985
Austria	24,793	173,215	5,207	78,593	21	45
Belgium	20,178	247,499	3,228	113,120	16	46
Denmark	18,283	116,319	4,388	57,380	24	49
Finland	14,470	127,976	5,354	62,467	37	49
France	139,593	1,255,538	47,462	626,986	34	50
Germany	134,700	1,550,211	27,301	646,631	20	42
Greece	21,055	181,901	5,053	88,963	24	49
Ireland	8,782	70,301	2,547	30,385	29	43
Italy	145,170	1,117,742	37,744	476,028	26	43
Netherlands	61,036	404,866	12,818	165,993	21	41
Norway	7,537	94,658	1,206	49,233	16	52
Portugal	24,236	103,585	7,204	55,599	30	54
Spain	55,272	935,126	7,729	459,105	14	49
Sweden	16,887	220,881	3,884	104,055	23	47
U.K.	133,759	1,032,491	45,226	469,945	24	46

Source: UNESCO Statistical Yearbook (1965: 260–63 and 1995: 3–269 through 3–277). "Education at the Third Level: Teachers and Students by Type of Institution." Data from 1950 unavailable for some countries; the nearest available data point has been substituted: Greece (1955) and Portugal (1960). For Italy, 1985 was substituted for 1980 for the same reason.

ucated; three-quarters of all ministers in postwar Europe have held university degrees (Blondel 1991). Further, the political elite overrepresent certain occupations. Blondel's (1991) data reveal that roughly half of all cabinet members have been lawyers (22 percent), teachers (19 percent), or civil servants (11 percent). Also present in the cabinets Blondel studies are sizable representations of industrialists and businessmen, farmers, professionals such as doctors, and leaders of interest groups, such as trade union officials and persons whose whole career has been devoted to politics.

In all fifteen of the countries that are the subject of this book, the number of women in university and university-equivalent programs grew phenomenally between 1950 and 1990 (table 3). Throughout Western Europe, both the male and female populations of students grew over this period, but the growth of male enrollment paled in comparison with the growth of women's.

The proportion of female college students rose from more or less one-quarter to nearly half the student population during 1950–90. In both Portugal and Norway, female college students have become a majority population. The Portuguese data are particularly astounding given that the revolution and subsequent transition to democracy occurred only twenty years ago.[1] The changes in the data reflect the profound transition undergone by Portuguese women. Under Salazar's rule, a man could murder his adulterous wife with impunity.[2] Further, domestic work was compulsory for women (Kaplan 1992).

Table 4. Women in the Workforce, 1950 and 1985

Country	Total Workforce		Female Workers		Percentage Female	
	1950	1985	1950	1985	1950	1985
Austria	3,347,115	3,355,200	1,299,252	1,323,900	38	39
Belgium	3,481,027	4,114,809	820,916	1,676,297	24	41
Denmark	2,063,401	2,752,961	694,426	1,254,050	34	46
Finland	1,984,282	2,444,679	808,229	1,153,350	41	47
France	19,171,340	24,085,300	6,663,480	9,937,300	35	41
Germany	22,174,457	29,012,000	8,368,680	11,433,000	38	39
Greece	2,839,481	3,892,457	510,580	1,379,501	18	35
Ireland	1,272,038	1,302,400	324,848	385,300	26	30
Italy	20,671,777	23,364,000	5,271,221	8,249,000	25	35
Netherlands	3,866,445	6,486,000	943,603	2,436,000	24	38
Norway	1,388,144	2,063,000	328,250	898,000	24	44
Portugal	3,288,452	4,695,700	737,063	1,955,500	22	42
Spain	10,793,057	13,345,500	1,708,830	4,091,800	16	31
Sweden	1,552,587	4,424,000	341,244	2,082,000	22	47
U.K.	23,213,404	26,350,000	7,143,737	10,315,000	31	39

Source: International Labour Organization, "Total and Economically Active Population by Sex and Age Group," in *Yearbook of Labour Statistics: Retrospective Edition on Population Census: 1945–1989* (Geneva: ILO, 1990), 78–110. Data from 1950 unavailable for some countries. The nearest available data point was used as an alternative: Austria (1951), Belgium (1947), France (1954), Greece (1951), Ireland (1951), Italy (1951), Netherlands (1947), U.K. (1951). Data from 1985 unavailable for some countries. The nearest available data point was substituted: Belgium (1987), Netherlands (1987), and U.K. (1980).

In both Portugal and Norway, the university populations are majority female, but Norway has one of the highest levels of women in cabinet positions, whereas Portugal has one of the lowest among the fifteen countries. This implies that the level of women in higher education either provides no explanation for the proportion of women in government or is only one of many factors that explains women's participation in government. The Pearson coefficient of correlation between the proportion of women in cabinet positions and the change in women's access to higher education is positive, but small ($r = .1681$), suggesting that although not irrelevant, educational access is only part of the explanation for women's level of participation in government.

Not only have European women begun to shatter men's monopoly on education, but they have also become much more integrated into their national economies. In each of the fifteen countries, the percentage of the workforce that was female increased during the postwar period, almost doubling in Belgium, Norway, Portugal, Spain, and Sweden. Women now make up no less that 30 percent of the workforce in any of these countries (table 4).

Many have suggested that increases in educational opportunities and workforce participation should bolster the political participation of women (Darcy, Welch, and Clark 1994; Anderson 1975; Verba, Nie, and Kim 1978; Studlar and Matland 1994). Analysis of the data, however, suggests that the educational and occupational opportunities that have opened up to women in the last thirty years are only nominally related to a change in women's level of representation in government.[3] The Pearson correlation coefficient for the relationship between women in government and the change in the number of women in higher education is .17; the relationship of women in government to the change in the workforce participation is even weaker, $r = .02$.

What accounts for these weak relationships? One explanation for the absence of a more significant relationship between university enrollment and political participation is found not in the numbers enrolled but in the type of educational programs into which women are channeled. European women are still concentrating upon a narrow range of subjects reflecting their traditional interests, such as nursing and education and the humanities, rather than the hard sciences and engineering (Christy 1984; Haavio-Mannila and Skard 1985; Norris 1987; Kaplan 1992). Even in the same classroom, however, men and women receive different educational experiences. Just as in the United States, educational instructors in Sweden, for example, pay greater attention to male students than to female students (Wistrand 1981; Kaplan 1992). In the workforce no less than in the educational sphere, a large degree of segregation persists, even in the Scandinavian countries thought to be notably egalitarian (Haavio-Mannila and Skard 1985; Kaplan 1992; Norris 1987; Togeby 1994). Norris (1987) refers to segregation among the European workforces as horizontal (by occupation) or vertical (within organizations). Educational and occupational segregation may limit women's participation in government because some professions—such as the legal profession and the civil service, in which women have been significantly underrepresented—are more likely than others to lead to political recruitment (Norris 1987; Kaplan 1992).

In addition, although governments have done a lot to alter the educational and occupational opportunity structures for women—particularly middle-class white women—the structure of domestic work has been significantly unaltered (Randall 1987; Norris 1987; Kaplan 1992). Studies have shown that the amount of time that men contribute to domestic work has increased in Denmark in the last twenty years. Even so, Danish women still spend almost two and one-quarter hours more per day on domestic work than do men (Togeby 1994). This results in a double burden that leaves women less able to translate their knowledge and skills into political capital. The degree to which part-time work is women's work is a testimony to the persistence of inequitable divisions of domestic work. Three-fourths of all part-time workers in the

European Union are female, and in Scandinavia, 80 to 90 percent of all part-time positions are filled by women (Kaplan 1992).

Another possible explanation points to a time lag. Some evidence suggests that it is not the current levels of educational enrollment and workforce participation but the levels of a generation earlier that influence the participation of women in government. Although the proportion of women enrolled in university degree programs in the 1950s is not related to the current participation of women in government, the proportion of women in the workforce in the 1950s is strongly related ($p = .5577$).

A time lag might result from the higher level of resources (education or occupational prestige) required of women than of men to achieve the same gains in the political realm. Finding that women's credentials for political office were generally higher than those of their male counterparts, Carroll (1984) argues that women are more stringently held to eligibility standards. The reason may be their association—by virtue of their sex—with feminism, a "conflict-producing societal group," thus making them "immediately suspect as outsiders" (Carroll 1984, 94). If, as Carroll argues, women are held to higher eligibility standards, educational and occupational attainment might not translate into the same rate of participation for women as for men.[4] Verba et al. (1978) refer to the translation of skill into political resources as the process of converting social into political capital. Espousing somewhat different reasoning, they too argue that the conversion of social capital into political capital is different for men and for women.

The notion of a time lag entails a belief in the inevitability of linear progression for women over time. In recent years, many have challenged this assumption, arguing that women's advancement in one realm often incites backlash in another (Kaplan 1992; Faludi 1991; Bystydienski 1988, 1992a).

Another reason that educational attainment and workforce participation are only weakly related to women's participation in government lies in the underrepresentation of women in European parliaments. The qualification for membership in the Western European political elite that women are most lacking, by far, is a seat in parliament.

Election to Parliament

Cabinet ministers are almost inevitably drawn from among the ranks of parliamentarians (Aberbach et. al 1981; Blondel 1991; de Winter 1991; Cotta 1991; Theakston 1987; Rose 1989). Although having a seat in parliament is not in most cases a constitutional requirement for cabinet membership, the political realities of parliamentary democracies make parliamentary election a de facto requirement.[5] Rewarding loyal party members with plum political appointments is one of political parties' primary ways of retaining party disci-

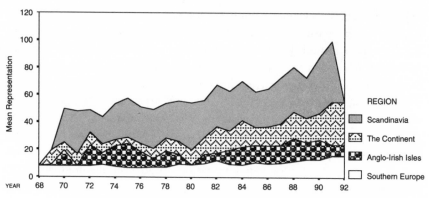

Figure 6. Women in Parliament by European Region, 1968–1992

pline (Calvert 1987). Further, since cabinets in parliamentary democracies are accountable to the parliaments, the appointment of a number of nonparliamentarians to the government risks a strain in relations between cabinet and legislature (Blondel 1991).

In addition, parliamentarians' talents are those most likely to come to the attention of the prime minister (Blondel 1991). Theakston (1987) argues that in the British system it is parliamentary performance that secures both an initial appointment to the government, usually as a junior minister, and subsequent promotion to cabinet rank. For this reason, Sinn Féin party leader Gerry Adams once scoffed at all British parliamentarians as being "unprincipled careerists jockeying for the ministerial Mercedes" (Majendie 1986).

If women are to be appointed to government, then, they must first be elected to parliament. It is this qualification for membership in the pool of eligibles, more than any other, that women lack. In 1991, women constituted 12.5 percent of all European parliamentarians (IPU 1991). Of course, that continental average masks a great deal of regional variation. In general, the patterns of women's participation in parliaments are similar to those in government: Scandinavian parliaments have the highest proportions of women, those in southern Europe the lowest, and those in the Anglo-Irish isles and continental Europe fall somewhere in between (fig. 6).

The clear correspondence between women's levels of representation in parliament and in government raises the question of whether their participation in government (or lack thereof) is explained solely by their presence (or absence) in parliament. The two are strongly related, but the processes by which representation in parliament translates into participation in government are not what descriptions of cabinet system recruitment processes might suggest.

Explaining Women's Government Participation

Because it is primarily parliamentarians who are appointed to government, we can expect to find that cross-national and party differences in women's participation rates in parliament will translate into cross-national and inter-party differences among participation rates of women in government.

We cannot, however, expect that current parliamentary participation rates will translate into current government participation rates. There are few freshmen government appointments (Theakston 1987). I thus postulate a lag between time of parliamentary intake and time of government appointment. This lag will be shorter for appointment to junior positions in government and longer for senior posts.

Chapter 4 elaborates more fully on the range of norms in patterns of recruitment to the cabinet. There is a substantial cross-national variation in "parliamentary waiting" times, that is, the average tenure that parliamentarians have before reaching the cabinet. In countries that have longer parliamentary apprenticeships, we would expect fewer women in cabinet positions. In these systems, women's historical absence from parliaments will translate into absence from government well into the future.

Positive Action and Positive Discrimination

Because there are so few women in parliament and because governments are under pressure to appear, at least, to be representative, some people have argued that women are actually advantaged in the process of political appointment (Darcy, Welch, and Clark 1994; Kohn 1980). Stuart Elaine MacDonald (1989) examines this possibility in an analysis of the promotion rates of British parliamentary members from backbencher to government whip, junior minister, and cabinet member.[6] MacDonald finds that women are in fact disadvantaged in the appointment process. The promotion rate for women is only three-fourths that for men among Conservative parliament members and only slightly better among Labour members (MacDonald 1989). MacDonald's research suggests that women's absence from government is related only in part to their underrepresentation in national legislatures.

I do not expect, therefore, women's presence in the parliamentary pool of eligibles alone to explain variation in rates of participation in government. In fact, I expect that women will not be present in government at even the rates suggested by their presence in the pool of eligibles, in part because of gender-related differences in the nature of parliamentary participation. I expect negative relationships between the patterns of gender-specific specialization within parliamentary committees, on the one hand, and the participation of women in government, on the other. Where women are less likely to maneuver in parliament—for example, by occupying several positions and demonstrating competence in a range of matters—they will be disadvantaged, particularly in systems that place a premium on parliamentary visibility.

Each of the gender differences outlined in this chapter—in background, in committee participation and in frequency of participation in plenary debates—has implications for the likelihood that the party elite will notice women and promote them to cabinet ranks. However, not all political systems tap their parliamentary pool for ministerial office in the same ways. Gender differences are more significant in some systems than in others. The following chapter examines the differences among political systems in the ways that cabinets relate to parliaments, thereby outlining the ways that gender differences in the parliamentary context disadvantage women in the process of appointment to the government.

4

Recruitment Norms: The Rules of the Game

Many have observed that there are differences among countries in the ways that elites are recruited, in the informal rules of the game (see, for example, Dogan 1989). In general, cabinet systems fall along a continuum, from those comprising primarily generalists on one end to those comprising a large number of specialists on the other (Blondel 1991).[1] Generalist ministers have broad political backgrounds, whereas specialists enter government to work in an area of particular expertise (Blondel 1991).

A substantial amount of parliamentary maneuvering—that is, service in several parliamentary positions and committee assignments while acquiring tenure—is a prerequisite for cabinet membership in cabinets that fall closer to the generalist prototype. Not only do generalist systems tend to recruit relatively high percentages of their ministers from among the ranks of parliamentarians, but also the nonparliamentarians appointed in generalist systems tend to be political insiders or party henchmen.

Specialist systems, on the other hand, are more permeable, recruiting fewer parliamentarians and more outsiders. Even in specialist systems, though, there is a significant reliance on the parliamentary pool for potential ministers. During the post–World War II era, three-fourths of all cabinet ministers have been recruited from their national parliaments (de Winter 1991). In the majority of all cases, then, ministers are recruited from parliament. The issues are those of degree—the extent of reliance on nonparliamentary experts—and of which skills exhibited by parliamentarians are valued and rewarded with promotion to cabinet rank.

In every cabinet system at any given time, there is a mix of ministerial backgrounds. As illustration, one study (Gerlich and Müller 1988, 145–46) distinguishes among three kinds of ministers in the Austrian cabinet system: Politicians, appointed because of their position in the party; politically based experts; and independent experts. Differentiation between generalist and specialist systems does not mean that specialization does not occur in generalist systems or that generalists do not serve in specialist systems.

The recruitment norms of Great Britain fall close to the generalist pole (in fact, only the Irish cabinet system is closer), with greater than 95 percent of ministers recruited from parliament, having an average of 12.2 years of parliamentary tenure. Yet two-time Prime Minister Harold Wilson (1964–70 and 1974–76) writes that an important skill for a prime minister is the ability to recall a colleague's specializations (Wilson 1976).[2]

Despite noting a need for the specializations of particular members, Wilson's account of British governance offers a defense of the generalist type. He argues that governments must be accountable and responsive to a broad range of interests and that only party insiders and loyalists can be fully aware of this need and fully able to fulfill this obligation: "Parliamentary democracy will be threatened, and parties atrophy, if ministerial appointments go increasingly to technicians and apparatchiks" (Wilson 1976, 32).

According to one MP, members of the House of Commons do specialize, "become an expert—in political terms of being an expert, which is not being an expert in real terms" (as quoted in Searing 1994, 104). Searing (1994) suggests that the extent of the specialization by MPs may correspond to their ambition for higher office. Those who are ministerial aspirants seem to have discerned that becoming familiar with the contours of some policy area is welcome but that overspecialization is politically fatal. Said one parliamentarian he interviewed, "What was Harold Wilson's specialty? . . . What was Hugh Gaitskell's? What are Michael Foot's, Tony Crosland's? Let's look at the people who've made it to the top. . . . What did these characters specialize in? Nothing" (95).

At the opposite end of the spectrum from Great Britain is The Netherlands. Accounts of the process of government formation and allocation of ministerial portfolios in The Netherlands reveal a very high degree of parliamentary involvement. By one account, parliamentary specialists in specific issue areas from each of the parties to a coalition are consulted on the person to be designated as the minister in charge of each issue area (de Winter 1991). The degree of parliamentary involvement in The Netherlands might make the reliance on nonparliamentarians to fill ministerial office seem a surprise. As de Winter (1991) explains, the number of nonpolitical appointees in Dutch cabinets is related to the practice of consociationalism.[3] Appointing nonpartisan technocrats "ensures that government is above politics" (49). As consociational practices in The Netherlands have declined since the late 1960s, so too has the tendency to recruit ministers from outside the parliamentary realm (de Winter 1991; Andeweg 1988a). Andeweg (1988b) points out the coincidence of timing such that reliance on political appointees outstripped reliance on technocrats for the first time in 1967, the date commonly associated with the demise of the politics of accommodation in The Netherlands. Currently, a majority of recruits for ministerial office come from the Tweede Kamer (Dutch parliament).

Appointment of nonparliamentary experts is in part a result of coalitional efforts to keep government above politics, as noted by Gerlich and Müller (1988, 146). In Austria, they maintain, portfolios are allocated to nonpartisan experts when the coalition has a desire either to neutralize politically sensitive issue areas or to undertake a nonpartisan approach.

There is a considerable degree of overlap between the specialist categorization here employed and consociationalism. *Specialist* is not synonymous with *consociationalist*, however. Along with The Netherlands, Sweden and Finland fall close to the specialist end of the continuum. Politics in both of these countries are highly consensual in nature (Larsson 1988; Nousiainen 1988). Indeed, in the Swedish decision-making process, opposition politicians as well as representatives of interest groups are frequently asked to participate in the royal commissions that draft much of the preparatory work of legislation (Larsson 1988). But neither Finland nor Sweden is consociationalist. Moreover, Belgium, a highly fragmented country, has engaged in consociationalist practices at a number of points in its troubled history (see Lijphart 1987). Yet Belgium is situated much closer to the generalist than the specialist end of the spectrum, as it recruits almost 87 percent of its ministers from among parliamentarians, and the average parliamentary tenure before promotion to cabinet rank is 7.6 years.

Of perhaps greater correspondence with the specialist designation than consociationalism is a strong bureaucratic tradition (Larsson 1988; Nousiainen 1988). In their conceptions of ministerial office, the more generalist systems emphasize the representative function whereas systems closer to the specialist pole emphasize an administrative function alongside the representative one (Blondel 1988). The bureaucratic, or administrative, nature of cabinet government in Sweden is sometimes seen in protests that ministers have too heavily exerted their influence on the boards and agencies, autonomous from ministries, that are charged with implementing policy. Ministers are to direct but not to rule these agencies (Larsson 1988).

The emphasis on representation over administration in generalist systems results in rewards for specific skills, such as prowess in parliamentary debate, that are not necessarily related to the capacity for effective administration (Theakston 1987). In generalist Great Britain, descriptions of the process by which a parliamentarian is initially appointed a junior minister and perhaps subsequently promoted to the rank of secretary of state, emphasize the importance of demonstrating competence in parliamentary debate (Theakston

1987; Searing 1994). Theakston (1987) argues that prime ministers are only haphazardly aware of the talents of junior ministers. They tend to hear only of the spectacular successes or the horrendous debacles.

An important way to win the notice of British prime ministers is through finesse in parliamentary debate (Theakston 1987; Searing 1994; Rose 1988). Ministerial aspirants are advised to seek out opportunities to speak not only in Commons (but not "overly frequently") but also outside the house, with the press and in constituency meetings. MPs are counseled to focus their interventions on "tormenting the brutes opposite" (Searing 1994, 101, 102).

The diaries of Barbara Castles, Labour minister in both of Harold Wilson's governments, are replete with references to her participation in parliamentary debate and her Labour colleagues' notice of it. As an opposition member during the leadership of Edward Heath, she writes:

I managed to intervene in Heath's speech with a question that roused the House: "If the Pay Board's report on relativities, which I understand is due out shortly, makes out a case for special cases to receive special payment, is the Government prepared to amend the pay code immediately?" Heath stalled, of course, but Elystan Morgan [Labour MP for Cardiganshire] whispered to me, "That is the key issue. We must pursue it." Later in Annie's Bar, Charles Taylor [Conservative MP for Eastbourne] of all people, insisted on buying me a drink, saying, "I have never heard an intervention go to the heart of the matter more than yours did today." And he went on to say that when I first came into the House he thought I was a bitch. Then as he got to know me he came not only to respect, but to like me. Well, well! I intend to try and speak tomorrow (Castles 1980, 22, describing 9 January 1974).

Similarly, Thatcher writes that she agonized prior to her maiden speech— which was unconventional in supporting a private member's bill that she successfully sponsored as one of her first acts in the House of Commons (Thatcher 1995).[4] For subsequent interventions in the house, she writes she went to great lengths to prepare for debate, and she describes the response to her comments by her party colleagues, the opposition, and the press (Thatcher 1995). By her recollection, the points scored in parliamentary debate significantly affected her political fortunes. Another parliamentarian refers to such scores as his "striking rate" (Searing 1994, 101).

The difference between generalist and specialist systems is significant not only for appointment of persons to ministerial office but also for the direction of their ministerial careers. In generalist systems, promotion usually entails moving from one ministerial area to another (Rose 1975, 1987; Theakston 1987; Dogan 1989). It is thought that a minister's competence in one functional area will readily translate into competence in another. Moreover, the experience developed through service in a number of functional areas serves to reinforce the generalist background that is valued (Theakston 1987). In a specialist system, however, a greater degree of functional specialization is a requisite, and movement within (as from junior to senior minister) rather than between ministries is not uncommon (Larsson 1988).

Another difference is that the cabinets of generalist systems tend to be much more hierarchical than those of specialist systems. The degree of hierarchy influences the promotion patterns of ministers within cabinets (Theakston 1987; Rose 1975, 1987). In Italy, the pattern is observed in the regularity with which a senior minister reaches office only after having served a stint as a junior minister (Dogan 1989). Similarly, in the United Kingdom, two-thirds of all senior ministers pay their political dues as junior ministers (Theakston 1987). Although the ministerial hierarchy is not as transparent in Ireland, where ministerial reshuffles are rare and government is small, several aspects of hierarchical organization have been noted there. For example, seating arrangements at cabinet meetings give certain issue areas preferential treatment, ministers of some portfolios make more frequent and more authoritative interventions than others, and the Taoiseach (prime minister) is clearly preeminent (Farrell 1988). It is uncertain whether the hierarchy is cause or effect of the recruitment norms of these systems.

Specialist systems are more open to political outsiders and newcomers by virtue of their more permeable recruitment patterns. They also seem to be more open in terms of willingness to allow the public access to information surrounding decision-making processes. The closed nature of the British system, owing much to the Official Governments Secrets Act, is a well-known feature of politics in Britain (Lovenduski 1986; Rose 1989). Similarly, the Irish executive is said to be exceedingly concerned with secrecy (Farrell 1988). At the specialist end, scholars of Sweden and Finland note the open nature of cabinet decision making (Nousiainen 1988; Larsson 1988). Both the recruitment to and the procedures of specialist systems, then, seem to be more open than those of generalist systems. It seems that recruitment and operation mirror one another.

Recruitment Norms and Women's Access

There are reasons to expect that women are less likely to hold positions of power in generalist cabinet systems than in specialist systems. First, generalist systems' nearly exclusive reliance on parliament for recruitment means that if a woman is to be appointed to the cabinet, she must first be elected to parliament. As discussed, women constituted a mere 12.5 percent of all European parliamentarians in 1991 (IPU 1991). The low levels of female parliamentary membership translate into low participation rates in government not only in the present but also well into the future. Given the long parliamentary waiting periods necessary for what elite theorists refer to as certification for eligibility for office, the simple fact of having been absent in the past ensures future exclusion.

Second, the differences noted in chapter 2 between male and female parliamentarians also have implications for their advancement to ministerial office. As noted, women tend to enter politics at a later age then men; late entry may rule out consideration of many women because they are not able to accumulate sufficient parliamentary tenure to be certifiable for promotion (Randall 1987; Searing 1994; MacDonald 1989). There is a political "biological clock"—to use a gendered metaphor—for all aspirants to political office, male and female (Searing 1994, 91).[5] MacDonald (1989) argues that this restriction is critical. Not only do participants have a limited amount of parliamentary career time in which to establish themselves as promotable but also, she finds, younger MPs are favored in the process of promotion from the outset.

Third, women are less likely to receive attention from the elite leaders responsible for promotion because women tend to participate in parliamentary debates less frequently. The reasons are found in their absence from positions of party and committee leadership and their concentration in a narrow range of committee areas that do not consume a lot of plenary debate time (Skard 1985). Women's more circumscribed participation in debate means that they are likely to be passed over in generalist systems, which place a premium on parliamentary performance.

Finally, many have argued that systems that are closed and secretive by nature perpetuate recruitment in elites' own image (Lovenduski 1986). Since women have historically been absent from this self-perpetuating group, this aspect of the generalist/specialist differentiation also disadvantages women in the process of recruitment.

In sum, I expect the participation of women in all cabinet systems to be related to their participation rates in parliament. However, I also expect the association between women in parliament and those in government to be stronger in generalist systems. Further, I expect the sectorization of women to contribute to their absence from government, especially among generalists.

Data

To properly place the systems in this study on the continuum from generalist to specialist, a single recruitment indicator was devised on the basis of three of the characteristics of ministers: percentage of ministers recruited from among the ranks of parliamentarians, percentage of ministers who are neither parliamentarians nor national party leaders, and average tenure of parliamentarians selected for ministerial office (see table 5).[6]

Table 5. Patterns of Recruitment of Government Ministers

Country	Percentage MPs	Percentage Outsiders	Average Seniority (Years)
Austria	67.7	20.2	8.2
Belgium	86.9	6.0	7.6
Denmark	78.8	5.5	9.7
Finland	62.4	16.9	10.3
France	68.9	16.3	7.5
Germany	73.6	11.7	7.7
Italy	94.3	2.4	9.1
Ireland	95.9	0.0	9.2
Netherlands	52.9	37.5	7.0
Norway	57.1	8.8	7.8
Sweden	61.3	21.0	9.1
U. K.	95.1	2.6	12.2

Source: Data from Lieven de Winter, "Parliamentary and Party Pathways to the Cabinet," in *The Profession of Government Minister in Western Europe*, ed. Jean Blondel and Jean-Louis Thiebault (London: Macmillan, 1991), 48. Copyright © 1991. Reprinted with permission of St. Martin's Press, Inc. Figures are post–World War II averages.

Values on the recruitment indicator were determined by summing the three variables. Adding the number of years of parliamentary tenure to the percentage of ministers recruited from parliament gives a fuller indicator of the role of parliament in spawning ministers than does the percentage of parliamentarians alone. Combining de Winter's indicator of the number of "outsiders" gives us information about pure technocrats rather than simply about nonparliamentary appointees. Generalist systems tend to recruit parliamentarians, and the nonparliamentarians recruited are party insiders. The outsider measure of pure technocrats is, therefore, an equally important determinant of how open or closed the recruitment process is. Before summing the outsider indicator, though, the percentage of outsiders was converted to the percentage of insiders, its opposite (100 – percentage of outsiders), so that the directionality of all variables was the same. The resultant sum is thus more meaningful.

The indicator of recruitment norms has a range of values, from 122.4 (held by The Netherlands) on the specialist pole, to 205.1 (Republic of Ireland) on the generalist extreme. Each country's place on the scale is given in table 6.

In measuring the sectorization of women in parliament, I was more constrained, as no data have been consistently reported on each of the cases across time. As a best-case measure, I include data from the IPU survey on the defense committee participation of female MPs. Defense committee participation is a crude, though useful, indicator of the degree to which female parliamentarians have moved into issue areas outside their traditional spheres of interest.

Table 6. Index of Recruitment Norms

Netherlands	122.4	↑	
Sweden	149.4		Specialist
Austria	155.7		
Finland	155.8		
Norway	156.1		
France	160.1		
Germany	169.6		
Denmark	183.0		
Belgium	188.5		
Italy	201.0		
U. K.	204.7	↓	Generalist
Ireland	205.1		

In the model I have lagged the participation rate of women in parliament by one or two electoral periods. As noted, the average tenure of parliamentarians before appointment to the cabinet in the systems in this study is between 7.0 (The Netherlands) and 12.2 years (United Kingdom). In between the time that a delegate is elected and the time that his or her talent is tapped for the government (seven or more years), at least one election has intervened. With the exception of Sweden (which allows for a maximum of three years between elections), none of the countries within this study allow for more than five years between parliamentary elections (see Gallagher et al. 1992, 176). Rarely is a parliamentarian appointed to the government, then, without an intervening election. The appropriate designation of the representation of women in the parliamentary pool of eligibles for government at any given time is not the number of women in parliament chosen in the most recent election but the number chosen in the election before that.

An example may help to clarify the concept of electoral lags in women's representation. John Major put together his first ministerial team, in which there were no women, in November 1990, on the heels of significant gains in the representation of women in the House of Commons. In the June 1987 elections, women had received 6.3 percent of the parliamentary seats, up from 3.5 percent in June 1983. But those women who were elected for the first time in 1987 had not acquired the requisite tenure to be considered for Major's cabinet, given that the average parliamentary wait time for ministerial recruitment in the United Kingdom is a preclusive 12.2 years. In this case, the first lag in the pool of eligibles was the representation of women following the June 1983 elections; the second lag was the representation of women following the May 1979 elections, when they won 2.9 percent of the seats. The incidence in which a newly elected MP is appointed to the government is rare.

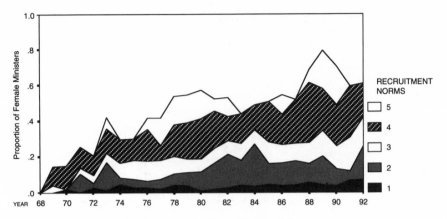

Figure 7. Women in Government by Recruitment Norms

Findings

The results of the analysis largely support expectations. There is a strong, negative relationship between a country's position on the generalist/specialist spectrum and the participation of women in government ($p = -.5337$). To depict this difference, the generalist/specialist indicator was collapsed into five categories. Note that the collapsed indicator is used solely for the purpose of graphing the differences among generalist and specialist systems. The interval level indicator is used in analysis that follows. For the collapsed indicator, countries were grouped so that The Netherlands, the most extreme on the specialist end of the spectrum, was given a value of 5. Extreme on the generalist end were Italy, the United Kingdom, and Ireland. They were given a value of 1. Other countries were grouped together in clusters of values such that Sweden, Austria, Finland, and Norway were assigned the value 2; France and Germany, 3; and Denmark and Belgium, 4. Note that these values reverse the direction of the first indicator. The first indicator assigned the highest value to the most generalist systems. The collapsed version assigns the highest value to the most specialist system.

Figure 7 depicts the sizable difference between generalist and specialist systems in the proportion of female ministers. The generalist systems indeed seem more difficult to permeate. But is this finding a result of the scarcity of women in parliament? Multivariate analysis reveals that it is not. Even when controlling for the presence of women in parliament, women seem to have a more difficult time accessing the highest ranks of the elite in generalist systems than in systems closer to the specialist pole (see table 7). Weighted least squares regression shows that women are much less likely to be promoted in generalist systems and that this is not explained by their presence in or absence from the parliamentary pool.[7] In other words, the recruitment norms

Table 7. Effect of Recruitment Norms on Women in Government

Variable	B	Std. Error
Intercept	−0.16	0.65
Size of Government		
Total Members***	0.15	0.01
Recruitment Norms		
Generalist[a]***	−0.02	0.00
Parliamentary Sectorization		
Defense Committee Participation***	0.06	0.01
Parliamentary Representation of Women		
Lag 1***	0.15	0.03
Lag 2*	−0.04	0.03
Region Differences/Political Culture		
Nordic	−0.06	0.24

$N = 455$
Adjusted $R^2 = .66$
$P > F = .00$

[a]The variable generalist has the values reported in table 2. The variable is ordered in such a way that specialist systems have the lowest values, generalist systems the highest.
* = Significant at the .10 level
** = Significant at the .05 level
*** = Significant at the .01 level

matter, just as had been expected. Women are disadvantaged in generalist systems. My model of women in government is very robust; it is able to explain more than 65 percent of the variation associated with the number of women in government.

In describing the participation of women in government and in parliament, I have noted consistent regional patterns such that the representation of women in Scandinavia far surpasses that in continental or southern Europe or the Anglo-Irish isles. Many have explained these regional patterns with reference to political culture (Inglehart 1981; Northcutt and Flaitz 1985; Norris 1987; Bystydzienski 1988, 1992; Rule 1986; Kaplan 1992).[8] It is widely believed that the egalitarian culture of Scandinavia results in higher levels of representation of women in the Nordic countries (Halsaa et. al 1985; Norris 1987; Kaplan 1992). It is important, therefore, to test or control for the effects of political culture.

There is not satisfactory variable of political culture with which to test the hypothesis.[9] Instead, I have placed in the model a dummy variable for the Nordic countries (Sweden, Finland, Norway, and Denmark).[10]

It is interesting that the Scandinavian dummy variable in the model is not statistically significant. It may well be that political culture matters and that Scandinavia has a political culture conducive to the inclusion of women. But the findings presented here challenge the oft-touted hypothesis of Scandinavian exceptionalism. From this analysis, it appears that the reason for higher representation levels of women in Scandinavia is not the open, egalitarian culture but the structure of the institutional environment of the political arena. Although this finding may surprise many, it is consistent with a growing body of literature that finds culture at best a partial explanation for the success of women in gaining office (Matland 1994a, 1994b, 1994c; Carty and Erickson 1991; Studlar and Matland 1994, 1996).

The idea that Scandinavia has high levels of representation because of an exceptionally egalitarian culture has always been subject to some criticism, most vocal on the part of those most familiar with the Scandinavian systems. Scholars of women's studies within the Nordic region refer to cultural exceptionalism as the "Scandinavian Myth" (Matland 1994c).

The notion that the political realm in Norway is free of sexist prejudice has been challenged in a variety of ways. Using an experimental design to examine the gender bias of Norwegian secondary school children, one study finds that gender stereotypes in evaluating candidate competencies in Norway are even greater than in the United States, where women have a significantly lower level of political representation (Matland 1994c). Other studies have shown that the ability of Norwegian voters at the local level to exercise preferential voting arrangements results in voter discrimination (Matland 1994a, 1994b, but see also Bystydienski 1988).[11] This suggests that there is sex discrimination in the Norwegian public among both youth and adults. Since women have been so successful in obtaining political office in Norway despite prejudice among the electorate, Matland (1994a, 1994b, 1994c) argues that women's success must be at least in part the result of institutional structures rather than of a more egalitarian political culture.

Further, there is significant variation within Norway in the success of women at gaining election to the national parliament. The variations have been found to have a clear association with varying intranational electoral structures, another indication of the inadequacies of cultural explanations (Matland 1994a, 1994b).[12]

Still others have criticized the cultural explanation on the grounds that women lack economic power rivaling their political power (Coleman 1994; Skjeie 1991; Dahlerup and Haavio-Mannila 1985; Eduards et al. 1985). Women throughout Scandinavia have been much less successful at accessing power in unions and in corporatist channels of decision making than they have been in the electoral realm (Skjeie 1991; Skard and Haavio-Mannila 1985a; Hernes and Hanninen-Salmelin 1985; Lovenduski 1986; Matland 1994b, 1994c).

The analysis presented here suggests limitations of explanations based on political culture. Although these findings are consistent with a growing body of work questioning an overreliance on cultural explanations for women's representation, caution is in order. Too much weight should not be attached to the findings presented here concerning political culture because of the crude way in which culture is operationalized. Instead, these findings should be taken as further evidence of a need to question rather than assume cultural import. The extent of the impact of political culture and the ways that cultural influences operate need further examination. One possible conclusion from the analysis presented here is that culture may operate through the normalization of recruitment patterns. Note the similarity between the openness of specialist recruitment norms as described here and those aspects of the Scandinavian culture thought to foster women's inclusion. If indeed culture has operated through the adoption of a specific cluster of recruitment patterns, this could be one explanation for the absence of an independent impact of culture in this model.

In contrast to the performance of the political culture variable, the defense variable performs very much as had been expected. Defense committee participation is positively related to the number of women in government. This finding confirms the expectation that it is not merely the level at which women participate in parliament but the nature of their participation that attracts the recognition of the party hierarchy that results in promotion to cabinet rank.

Some interesting differences arise when the data are disaggregated by recruitment norms. The model is based primarily on parliamentary representation. In the specialist systems, however, many members of the government are appointed from outside the ranks of parliament. In the case of specialist systems, is the model useful in explaining women's participation in government?

Disaggregated Analysis

Rather than analyzing the data country by country, I have disaggregated the data into generalist and specialist systems to more clearly distinguish the differences between the two. For the purposes of disaggregating the data, those countries that were given a value of 1 or 2 on the specialist indicator used in figure 7 (The Netherlands, Austria, Sweden, Finland, Norway) were considered specialist. Those countries with a value of 4 or 5 on the specialist indicator (the United Kingdom, Italy, Ireland, Denmark) were designated as generalist. Germany and France, which have middling positions on the spectrum, have been excluded from the following analysis. Note that this division into generalist and specialist systems crosscuts the Nordic region, with Denmark falling into the generalist category and Austria and The Netherlands into the specialist one.

There are significant differences in the performance of the model as a whole and in the explanatory power of several of the variables between the two systems. Although the model is powerful in both subgroups of the data, it per-

Table 8. Predictors of Women in Government: Generalist Systems

Variable	B	Std. Error
Intercept***	15.15	3.96
Size of Government, Total Members	0.01	0.02
Recruitment Norms Generalist***	−0.07	0.02
Parliamentary Sectorization/ Defense Committee Participation	−0.03	0.05
Parliamentary Representation of Women		
Lag 1	−0.02	0.04
Lag 2**	0.10	0.04
Region Differences/Political Culture Nordic	−0.30	0.47

$N = 158$
Adjusted $R^2 = .63$
$P>F = .00$

Note: Generalist systems include the United Kingdom, Ireland, Belgium, and Denmark. The dependent variable is the number of women in government.
* = Significant at the .10 level
** = Significant at the .05 level
*** = Significant at the .01 level

forms best in the generalist system (see tables 8 and 9). This finding is not unexpected. The model takes into account only variables associated with the parliament. It should therefore perform better in those systems that are more closely tied to parliament—the generalist types. The model is powerful in both subgroups because even in specialist systems, the majority of all ministers receive their training in the parliamentary arena.

The percentage of women in parliament is a significant explanatory variable in all systems. Differences in the ways that the lagged variables of women's electoral representation perform in the two types of systems confirm important distinctions concerning parliamentary tenure. In the generalist systems, the first lag (women's electoral representation following the prior election) is not a relevant explanatory factor. Only the representation of women two electoral periods prior is influential in the generalist population. The longer parliamentary wait times among generalist types are a significant way in which women, by virtue of being absent in the past, are excluded well into the future.

In the specialist systems, in contrast, the level of representation of women in parliament during the prior electoral period is a very strong, positive predictor of their governmental access. Governments of the specialist category appear to be quickly translating the parliamentary expertise of women into governmental expertise. Further, the representation of women in parliament two electoral periods earlier is also statistically significant, at the .10 level.

Table 9. Predictors of Women in Government: Specialist Systems

Variable	B	Std. Error
Intercept**	8.95	4.02
Size of Government		
Total Members***	0.14	0.01
Recruitment Norms		
Generalist/Specialist***	−0.07	0.02
Parliamentary Sectorization/		
Defense Committee Participation**	0.04	0.02
Parliamentary Representation of Women		
Lag 1***	0.26	0.05
Lag 2*	−0.10	0.06
Region Differences/Political Culture		
Nordic***	−1.73	0.41

$N = 191$
Adjusted $R^2 = .57$
$P>F = .00$

Note: The specialist systems are Austria, The Netherlands, Sweden, Norway, Finland. The dependent variable is the number of women in government.
* = Significant at the .10 level
** = Significant at the .05 level
*** = Significant at the .01 level

The negative relationship found between women in government and women in parliament, lagged twice, may reflect some of the efforts, noted by others, at positive action, or positive discrimination. Women may be benefiting from government efforts to incorporate them in such a way that women are over-represented in government in comparison with their presence in parliament historically (two electoral periods earlier). Alternately, a significant influx of women into parliament in most European systems during the 1980s may account for these negative relationships. In this case, the data would reflect levels of parliamentary representation so significantly greater than prior levels that representation in government could not possibly match them. Change does not appear, though, to be occurring in such a rapid fashion, so the first interpretation is probably merited.

The disaggregated analysis continues to confound the political culture hypothesis. The Nordic variable is not statistically significant in the generalist subgroup. Denmark, having one foot in Scandinavia, one foot on the European continent, is the only Scandinavian country in the generalist subgroup.[13] It appears that the Nordic influence in Denmark does not give Danish women an advantage over women in other generalist systems. When controlling for other factors, the Nordic political culture does not appear to contribute positively to the promotion of women in the specialist subgroup either. The average level of parliamentary participation of women in Scandinavia during this time frame is just slightly greater than 25 percent. This is significantly greater than the average representation levels in the other three regions in this study (roughly 5 percent in the Anglo-Irish isles, just over 6 percent in southern Europe, and just over 8 percent on the continent). When controlling for this sizable recruitment pool, there is no additional advantage for Scandinavian women. In fact, in comparison with the ways that parliamentary participation translates into cabinet participation in other specialist systems, women in Scandinavia are underrepresented. The Scandinavian political culture may play a role in creating the eligibility pool, for example, by influencing the numbers of women who seek elected office. But the egalitarian nature of the Nordic region does not account for women's representation at the apex of political power.

It is notable that even within the subgroups, differentiations along the generalist/specialist continuum effect the likelihood that women will be recruited to government. The more open the system, the greater the chances that women will succeed in reaching office. I can suggest that the rules of the game, the recruitment norms of a cabinet system, taken together with the findings concerning political culture, are one of the most significant explanations for women's presence in or absence from government.

A final difference between the two groups of countries concerns women's participation in defense committees. Whether or not women participate in significant numbers in issue domains outside the realm of traditional women's values but inside the realm of matters on which parliament spends significant amounts of time its relevant in explaining the number of women in government in specialist systems. The defense committee participation variable is statistically strong, positive, and significant in the specialist model, even after controlling for the level of women in parliament. In the generalist systems, however, defense committee participation is not a significant explanatory factor.

Defense committee participation can be seen partly as a proxy measure of women's involvement in those matters that engage significant portions of parliaments' attention. The more likely women are to participate in nontraditional areas—such as defense—the more likely they are to be more centrally involved in parliamentary business, including parliamentary debate. It has been argued that women's concentration in a narrow range of issue areas means that they participate in debate less frequently. I expected the extent of participation in parliamentary debate to influence women's chances of recruitment in generalist systems, since they reward general political skills such as the ability to score points in debate. Therefore, inasmuch as extent of participation in defense committees is also an indicator of intercession in parliamentary debate, I expected such participation to be relevant to the chances of women's recruitment in generalist systems only. I did not expect participation in parliamentary debate to be similarly influential in specialist systems. Specialist systems value and reward a different set of skills.

In this case, why are the findings different from what had been expected? Why does defense committee participation matter in the specialist systems, but not in the generalist category? One explanation may lie in the virtual absence of variation in the participation in defense committees among the generalist subgroup. In both Italy and the United Kingdom, no women were members of the defense committees. In Belgium, women accounted for a mere 4.3 percent. Only in Denmark was there a sizable number of women on the defense committees in the generalist systems.

A possible explanation is found within organization theory. Beginning with Rosabeth Moss Kanter (1977), scholars have devoted a lot of attention to the performance of minority group members in institutional settings characterized by a majority culture. Kanter elaborates a typology based on the extent of representation of the minority group within the institutional setting. In her typology, institutional settings in which the minority culture is completely excluded are *uniform*; when the minority population has a representation level of 15 percent or less (but more than zero), the settings are *skewed*; with a balance between minority and majority groups approaching 35:65, the setting is *tilted*; finally, where there is parity or distribution along the lines of 40:60, the two cultures are more or less *balanced*.

The women in Kanter's study, members of a skewed Fortune 500 sales team, labored under significant handicaps. Here I outline but a few. The female sales representatives were subjected to stereotyping, heightened performance pressures (by virtue of their acts having "symbolic consequences" for the rest of their sex), and visibility problems. The visibility problems were dual in nature. On the one hand, the female salespersons were subjected to heightened scrutiny. No detail of their personal lives or appearance escaped the notice of their peers, their supervisors, or their clientele. On the other hand, their technical abilities, accomplishments, and credentials received scant notice. In other words, their merit was eclipsed by their auxiliary traits (Kanter 1977). Women in skewed institutional settings tend to respond to the problems associated with their "token" status by blending in, becoming less visible, speaking less frequently, demonstrating loyalty to the dominant group, and distancing themselves from other members of their sex (Kanter 1977; Spangler et al. 1978).

Among the cases in my study, only 4.5 percent of all cabinet changes in the generalist system took place against the backdrop of a "balanced" parliamentary chamber, whereas 82.7 percent occurred in a skewed setting. In contrast, in the specialist system, 24.8 percent of all appointments were answerable to balanced parliaments and only 28.9 percent were made in a skewed setting (see table 10).

Table 10. Institutional Balance by Recruitment Norms

Col %	Generalist	Neither	Specialist
Skewed	82.7	88.1	28.9
Tilted	12.8	11.9	46.3
Balanced	4.5	0.0	24.8
Total %	100.0	100.0	100.0
	(156)	(84)	(121)

$X^2 = 115.5, DF = 4$

Note: See tables 8 and 9 for lists of generalist and specialist systems. Germany and France are neither generalist nor specialist. Following the work of Kanter (1977), skewed parliaments are those in which women comprise 0 to 15 percent of the membership; in tilted parliaments, women comprise more than 15 percent but less than 30 percent; and in balanced parliaments women hold at least 30 percent of the seats.

In the generalist systems, the very unbalanced distribution of seats between men and women may render meaningless the participation of the few women represented in nontraditional committee areas. Women in generalist systems may be so constrained by their token status that their presence on these committees is not a meaningful indicator of their participation in parliament.

Conclusion

This analysis has shown that the distinction between generalist and specialist types of cabinet systems is indeed a useful one. Others have shown that there are significant differences between the patterns by which these two types recruit members. These differences are significant in explaining the cross-national variation in the participation of women in government. In fact, the recruitment norms—the rules of the political game—are one of the most significant explanatory factors for women's presence or absence among the ranks of the highest elite.

Once it is controlled for the institutional norms, political culture appears to have little impact. This finding augments recent research that has suggested culture to be at best a partial explanation for women's success in accessing political power. Instead, there appear to be clear institutional explanations for the presence of women in government in both generalist and specialist cabinet systems. One possibility is that culture is an underlying variable. The more egalitarian political cultures may foster recruitment processes more open to all political outsiders—male and female alike—and it may be this openness from which women benefit.

This analysis confirms that generalist systems are less permeable than specialist types for all persons, not only women. Entrance to government in a generalist system is preceded by a lengthy parliamentary waiting period. The effect is that women and other groups who were not present in the parliament in the past are absent from government well into the future.

The specialist-type systems provide a significant contrast to the generalist pattern of recruitment, being much more permeable for women and others. This permeability results in higher rates of participation for women. In specialist systems, participation in the parliament is one path to government but not the only one. Moreover, a long parliamentary apprenticeship is not the norm in these systems. The greater openness and the shorter parliamentary consignments of these systems suggest explanations for the dynamism of observed change in representation of women in government. Women's historical absence in specialist-type parliamentary arenas does not manifest itself in absence from higher political office for an extended period of time, as in the generalist systems. Changes in life opportunities for women that result in the election of women to parliament in these societies quickly translate into opportunities to govern. Moreover, it is often changes in life opportunities for women that result in changes in electoral representation levels. Because specialist systems recruit outside parliamentary channels, expertise in many fields can be tapped for government service even if that expertise has not first been translated into parliamentary representation.

Specialist systems' oppenness benefits women as well as men. This does not mean, however, that men and women have equal chances of promotion in specialist systems, even given equal representation and tenure in parliament. As the findings concerning defense committee participation in the pooled and specialist models show, women will be disadvantaged in the processes of recruitment either as long as they continue to specialize in a narrow range of parliamentary matters or as long as advanced industrial societies continue to place less value on the matters in which women have traditionally specialized. As long as the fields in which women specialize—health, education, welfare—are accorded less parliamentary attention, women will have fewer opportunities in specialist systems to demonstrate their competence and therefore diminished chances for promotion.

This analysis suggests that some of the obstacles women face in obtaining government positions are no different from those faced by any other entrants to the political system. Other barriers, however, are gender-specific.

Common to both the specialist and generalist systems is a strong reliance on the parliamentary channel of recruitment. This analysis therefore indicates that significant change in women's representation in government in all countries necessitates change in their participation in other levels of the formal political arena as well. Access to the highest ranks of political power requires access to the lower rungs and participation in a way that certifies eligibility for the highest ranks.

5

The Party-Parliament Nexus

Blondel (1985) describes the path to government in Western European systems as the "Parliamentary-cum-Party" route. It is by working one's way up through the ranks of the parliamentary party that one can be rewarded with ministerial appointment.[1] Once a coalition deal is struck, decisions are made on which portfolios to allocate to which party. Political parties then allocate these portfolios among their faithful.

In general, political parties enjoy a great deal of autonomy in deciding how to apportion their share of the cabinet spoils among their political faithful (Nousiainen 1988). We would therefore expect the participation of women in each party's parliamentary party to be the strongest predictor of women's success in recruitment to the cabinet. By taking into consideration the political party, we can refine and improve the model of appointments presented in chapter 4.

Even within the same political system, political parties participate in cabinet government differently. Political parties vary in the length of ministerial duration (Frognier 1991), the degree of interest in portfolios (Keman 1991), and the experiences they value when selecting ministers (Theakston 1987).

Where women are concerned, scholars have treated political parties of the left and the right separately because of the widespread belief that parties of different ideological hues have dissimilar perspectives on the role of women in the political arena, some being more willing than others to elect and appoint women.[2] Specifically, there is a widespread belief that parties on the political left are more egalitarian than those on the right (Duverger 1955; Lovenduski 1986; Skard and Haavio-Mannila 1985a; Norris 1987; Togeby 1955).

François Mitterrand's election as president in France after years of rule by the political right was heralded as "a breath of fresh air" for women (Kaplan 1992, 170).[3] One of Mitterrand's first acts was to rescue the women's ministry from oblivion. He resurrected the post of secretary of state for the condition of women that Giscard d'Estaing had created in 1974 and subsequently abolished. The ministry's new title (minster of women's rights), referring to the "rights" rather than the "status" of women, was indicative of the government's greater commitment to women (Kaplan 1992). Also indicative was the size of the ministry's budget: ten times that of its predecessor.

Parties of the left have historically taken the lead in promoting the interests of women. They have generally been more willing to make agreements with women's organizations on greater opportunities for political participation, and they have been better able to follow through on those commitments (Lovenduski 1993). In Greece, for example, where scholars have noted that neither parties of the left nor those of the right have been particularly attentive to the inclusion of women in decision-making bodies, it was nonetheless the Socialist regime of the 1980s that spearheaded efforts to liberalize abortion law and reform patriarchal family law that declared husbands the head of the family (Norris 1987).

Scholars of Western European party systems have noted that many rightist parties are confessional, for example, the Christian Democrats, which tend to have traditional notions about the role of women. Western European parties of the left, in contrast, are often worker oriented. Leftist parties are viewed as having more egalitarian views toward all persons—men and women alike (Norris 1987). Some have gone so far as to refer to European leftist parties as institutions of affirmative action (Aberbach et al. 1981, 59).

Some evidence of the tendency for leftist parties to be more willing than parties of the right to share power with women comes from Great Britain. Some have observed that the Labour Party is slightly more likely to slate women for safe seats than is the Conservative Party (Hills 1981; Studlar and Welch 1992).[4] The Conservative Party has been shown to be more likely to nominate women in metropolitan borough elections, but Conservative female candidates have less chance of winning (Studlar and Welch 1992). This finding suggests that Conservative Party women are nominated as "sacrifical lambs" (Brodie 1985). Others note that the Labour Party is more aware of the need for inclusiveness in the formation of cabinets (Rose 1971).[5]

Although it has been frequently suggested that parties of the left tend to be more favorably disposed than those of the right to sharing leadership with women, scholars are not unanimous on this point.[6] The history of organized labor's relationship to feminism has been conflictual, and the primacy of class conflict has meant that concerns about gender equality have frequently been subjugated (Graves 1994; Evans 1987; Norris 1987; De Beauvoir 1984; Beckwith 1985; Einhorn 1993).

Further, recent work cites evidence from Scandinavia, Canada, and West Germany that parties of the right are no less willing than parties of the left to

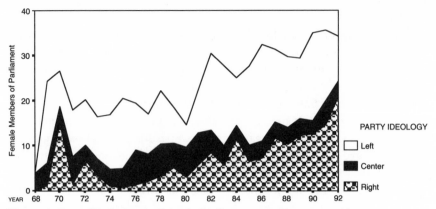

Figure 8. Party Variation in Female Parliamentary Representation

nominate and elect women (Darcy et al. 1994; Coleman 1994; Studlar and Matland 1994). In Canada, for example, it was not until the surprising electoral victory of the Conservative Party in 1984 that a sizable proportion of women came into office (Studlar and Matland 1994). Party ideology may no longer be a reliable indicator of inclusiveness (Lovenduski 1993).

Norris (1987) notes that the question of whether parties themselves affect women's chances is a part of the larger debate about the impact of political parties on policy (see Rose 1984; King 1981). During the 1970s and 1980s, scholars amassed a great deal of evidence to suggest that parties have only a limited capacity to affect policy outcomes (Dye 1976; Jackman 1980, 1987; Rose 1984; King 1981; but see also Lange and Garrett 1985, 1987; Cameron 1982, 1984). Instead, these scholars argued that economic and sociocultural factors associated with industrialized nations are determinant of political outcomes.

In discussing the second wave of feminism, Lovenduski (1993) notes that political parties of both left and the right have come under pressure to respond to the demands of their female constituents, members, and activists. One of their demands is greater inclusiveness of women by the parties. During the time frame of this study, gender became an explicit issue in many political parties across Europe.

If leftist parties have been more likely to appoint women to office, it may be a function of supply rather than of demand (Norris and Lovenduski 1992; Studlar and Matland 1994).[7] The vast majority of female parliamentarians have represented leftist parties (see figs. 8 and 9). As noted, it is through the parliamentary party that ministers are recruited. We would, given the greater supply of female parliamentarians on the left, expect more leftist female ministers.

Still other scholars have argued that it is not position on the left/right political spectrum but a party's size and status that determine its willingness to promote women (Lovenduski 1993; Brodie 1985; Studlar and Matland 1994,

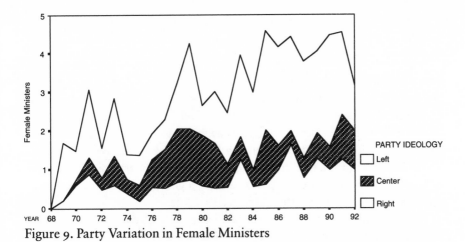

Figure 9. Party Variation in Female Ministers

1996; Ranney 1965; Hernes 1984; Bysydzienski 1988; Kolinsky 1991). For example, it has been the Greens in Germany who have led the way (Kolinsky 1991). Small parties' leadership may be a pragmatic rather than a philosophical matter. If the British Liberal Party leads in the nomination of women, the reason may be that it is more in need of feminist support (Lovenduski and Randall 1993; Hernes 1984; Skard and Haavio-Mannila 1985a) or that it is not in a position to be as "choosey" as the Labour and Conservative Parties (Ranney 1965).

If smaller parties' greater willingness to slate women for competitive seats in electoral contests is a result of their difficulty in fielding candidates rather than of their interest in attracting female voters, then the pattern observed in electoral contests may not hold in this analysis of the process of appointments. In the analysis of appointments, I control for the percentage of women in the party's pool of eligibles—that is, the proportion of female MPs. I thereby control for the party's ability to field candidates. Any persistence of the pattern of smaller parties having greater rates of promotion of women would appear, then, to be the result of smaller parties' attempts to differentiate themselves from more mainstream ones.

The expectations, then, are that the number of women that a political party appoints to government is positively related to the number of women in its parliamentary party. For this reason, I would expect that political parties of the left have higher participation rates of women in the governments they form. However, because of recent scholarship on parts of continental and northern Europe, the relationship between left/right position and the recruitment of women may be weaker in recent years than it has been historically. The higher participation rates of women of leftist parties may be a result simply of their historically higher rates of representation in parliament, or it may be the result of an ideological position that is more inclined to promote women. I further expect that smaller political parties may have additional incentives to promote women that will manifest themselves in a negative relationship between vote share and appointment of women.

Data and Methods

For the purposes of this analysis, the unit of analysis is altered. Because the study seeks to clarify factors that motivate *individual* coalition partners to promote women, the unit of analysis is *each* party or coalition partner in a government. This unit of analysis allows discussion of the behavior of specific parties in the coalition, thereby testing for the effects of party-specific factors such as ideological position. If, for example, a government comprises three coalition partners, each partner is treated as a case.

The time frame for measurement of each unit of analysis is the point at which a change occurred in the composition of the cabinet. Each time there was a change in the government composition, then, information on each of the coalition partners was coded. The resultant number of cases is 1,039.

The dependent variable is the number of women in government for each coalition participant (party) and is thus different for each coalition partner in the government for any one period of time.

Data on the number of female MPs by political party were obtained by writing the secretariats of each of the parliaments as well as all parties of government. (See appendix 2 for a list of parliaments and parties that responded to the request for information.) Where discrepancies occurred between the information provided by the party and that provided by the parliament, the parliament's figures were used, on the grounds that they were a more uniform source of information within each country. Additionally, data on women in parliament as a whole for each country were provided by the IPU.[8]

For purposes of comparability, identification of the ideological complexion of political parties and of governments was based on the prior work of others. To classify governments, the Composition of Party in Government index used by the European Consortium project was used (Woldendorp, Keman, and Budge 1993). Individual political parties were placed according to Castles and Mair's (1984) ascriptions. Castles and Mair's expert judgments were supplemented with a variety of sources since the parties that their project placed on a left/right continuum did not include all parties of government in this study. The primary source with which their work was supplemented was McHale's (1983) encyclopedia of European political parties. (See appendix 1 for a list of political parties and their ideological placement.)

Findings

There is evidence that parties of the political left are more egalitarian than parties of the right, but the evidence is far from clear. Equal in importance to a

Table 11. Left/Right Postion and Female Participation in Government
(Correlation Coefficients)

Time	r
1968–70	.29
1971–72	.16
1973–74	−.01
1975–76	.17
1977–78	.13
1979–80	.19
1981–82*	.10
1983–84*	.24
1985–86*	.34
1987–88*	.27
1989–90*	.30
1991–92	−.18

* = Significant at the .05 level.

party's parliamentary participation by women in explaining its promotion of women to government, though, is another factor: the participation in parliament of women from all political parties.

A first look at the data suggests that there is some validity to questions about the strength of relationships between party ideology and the advancement of women. Pearson correlation coefficients between the composition of party in government and women in government are paltry ($r = .003$).

When the data are disaggregated by year, though, the relationship changes. There are several time periods in which the relationship between parties of the left and the participation of women in government is stronger and is statistically significant. Interestingly, in the most recent time period, 1991–92, the relationship is opposite what it has historically been, in that political parties of the right are actually more likely than parties of the left to promote women to office. This relationship is not statistically significant, however (see table 11). The fact that the period of rightist governments' leadership in the recruitment of women is not statistically significant may suggest that governments of the right have felt a need to catch up with, but not to surpass, the initiatives of leftist governments. Is the recruitment of women a cause that the right has attempted to embrace, in an effort to compete for—or at least not to be excluded from—the egalitarian label?

Alternately, might coalitional exigencies be the reason why the ideological complexion of government often seems so insignificant? There are several periods in which the ideological hue of government is unrelated to the participation of women in government. There are many reasons to believe that the nature of coalition bargaining and formation might dilute the leftist parties' commitment—or power—to recruit women. Some have argued that women benefit from more centralized decision-making mechanisms (Darcy, Welch, and Clark 1994; Norris 1993; Matland 1994b). The nature of the coalition, however, decentralizes power, since it includes at least two political parties and two decision-making centers. Further, political parties appoint their top personnel to head government ministries, and a single-party government leaves the spoils of office undivided. A coalition, in contrast, decreases the share of spoils each party enjoys. With fewer posts to award, a party participating in a coalition will be able to promote to office fewer of its party notables, fewer of the party faithful; women may be more likely to enjoy only the leadership positions that are lower on the rungs of the party ladders.

A Multivariate Model of Women in Government

In an effort to tease out of the data the answers to some of these questions, multivariate analysis was performed. To determine whether or not parties of the left were more likely to promote women to the cabinet, measures of both the party's left/right position and the coalition's left/right position were placed in the model.[9] This test would not highlight an independent effect of ideology if I were not also controlling for the number of women in the parliamentary party. Measures on the party's current female representation in parliament were added to the model. Lags (by electoral period) of this measure were also added, in the belief that the time-lagged measures of a party's female representation would most likely be the appropriate indicator of the party's number of women in government (since parliamentary service is usually viewed as a requirement for cabinet measurement). Similarly, measures of the overall representation of women in parliament, lagged one and two time periods, as well as the number of women from the coalition in the parliament, lagged one, two, and three time periods, were placed in the model.

To test the hypothesis related to a party's size, the party's share of the vote in the last election was used. Each party's share of the government seats was also introduced as a control variable, with the idea that parties that received fewer seats in the cabinet would also be inclined to appoint fewer women to the cabinet.[10] Additional control variables introduced include the type of government in which the party participated (whether, for example, it was a coalition and, if so, whether majority or minority coalition), as well as two measures of time. One measure was designed to capture the trend effects of time in the model. The second was a dummy variable for the compositional change in the government that occurred—that is, whether or not it was the result of a new government formation or a more minor change, such as a reshuffle. The change variable was designed to capture any "seasonal" effects in the model.[11] The analysis presented here is a weighted least squares analysis.[12] In light of findings reported in chapter 4, I have also included the interval-level variable

Table 12. Predictors of the Recruitment of Women, 1968–1992

	B	Beta
Left/Right Position		
Government/Coalition**	.14	.18
Party	.05	.05
Government Characteristics		
Type of Government***	−.17	−.20
Coalition (number of parties)	.04	.07
Female MPs: Government/Coalition		
Lag 1	−.04	−.33
Lag 2***	−.08	−.51
Lag 3*	.01	.10
Female MPs: Parliament		
Lag 1	−.01	−.05
Lag 2**	−.07	−.37
Female MPs: Party		
Current Representation*	.04	−.31
Lag 1*	−.05	−.31
Lag 2	−.03	−.16
Lag 3	.01	.02
Party Size/Strength		
Total Party Representation in Gov't**	.01	.15
Party's Vote Share**	−.02	−.17
Timing		
Year	.00	.00
Change in Government	−.02	−.01
System Characteristics		
Political Culture***	1.12	.53
Generalist/Specialist***	−.01	−.28

Adjusted R^2 = .48 F = 51.97
N = 1039   Sig F = .00

* = Significant at the .10 level
** = Significant at the .05 level
*** = Significant at the .01 level

to capture recruitment norms (the generalist/specialist variable) and a dummy variable for Scandinavia (to capture any effects of the Scandinavian political culture).

The results (table 12) reveal that the picture is much more complicated than had originally been conceptualized.

Party, Parliament, and the Constraints of Coalition

Contrary to expectations about women's representation in government being related to their representation among their party's parliamentary party, I find that the number of female parliamentarians from all political parties is an equally effective predictor of the number of women in government. Within a party, there is a relationship between women members in parliament and in government, but it is weaker than the relationships between all female MPs and all female ministers. In other words, whether or not a party appoints women to government seems to depend on the number of women parliamentarians from outside the party as much as—if not more than—the number who are party members. Why might this finding, contrary to expectations, occur?

Again, as in chapter 4, the work of organization theorists may prove useful. The power of a parliament's total number of female deputies as a predictor of the number of women that any given political party appoints to the cabinet might be either the power of the—often imputed but seldom proved—critical mass or a "contagion effect."

A contagion effect (Mohr 1982) might be said to occur if one party begins to recruit a greater number of women because another party within its party system has begun to do so (Matland and Studlar 1996). A contagion effect, then, is a response of one party to the behavior of other parties within its party system. A contagion effect might also occur if one party witnesses that another has adopted a policy that is electorally advantageous or, at a minimum, not electorally disadvantageous (Matland and Studlar 1996).

Matland and Studlar (1996) have suggested that the smaller parties within party systems begin this process, perhaps for some of the reasons outlined in the discussion of party size. Smaller parties may have additional reasons to cultivate feminist support, for example. Alternately, larger parties may be less willing to nominate and appoint women in the absence of clear evidence of voter support for such policies.

The process of contagion might spread faster in those systems that are highly competitive. The presence of several viable parties gives women activists a number of grounds upon which to argue for better representation. Not only can women in competitive systems make demands for representation based on equity grounds, but also they can argue that it is in the party's electoral interest (Matland and Studlar in press). Further, party competition in and of itself has been shown to play a role in the advancement of women's representation (Studlar and Welch 1992; Studlar and Matland 1994).

Critical mass is a term borrowed from the natural sciences that refers to the quantity of an entity need to spark an irreversible process of change. Dahlerup (1988) suggests several ways in which a critical mass might change the institutional environment of a parliament, most notably the willingness of a minority to mobilize the resources of the organization or institution to improve the situation for themselves and other minority groups (296). Indeed, anecdotal evidence suggests that this process is at work and that it is affecting specifically the composition of cabinet governments. In Finland in the early part of 1989, when women's share of parliamentary seats had topped 30 percent, ten women's organizations affiliated with the Social Democratic Party forced the party to abandon a routine effort to dismiss a female minister.

This analysis shows that women's presence in the parliament—even the presence of women in nongovernmental parties—increases the likelihood of women being appointed to government. Similarly, the participation of women in other parties of government is a powerful predictor of the number of women that a party promotes. This is evidence of political parties promoting women in ways that suggest coalitional constraints or norms.

There is further evidence that such is the case. Women are more likely to be put forward in single-party majority governments than in minimum winning coalitions, and the same is more likely in minimum winning coalitions than in surplus majority coalitions.[13] Arguably, there is nothing a priori advantageous to women about centralized decision-making structures.[14] Both the will and the ability to recruit women must be present. Nonetheless, this analysis suggests that, controlling for ideology, there is a heightened ability to balance gender considerations in more centralized decision-making structures.

Ideology

A party's position on the left/right spectrum does not appear to play a role in the appointment of women. After controlling for a party's female delegation, the ideology of the party shows no independent effect on whether or not women are promoted to office. If the left has played a leadership position in the appointment of women, the explanation is the larger delegation of female parliamentarians on the left. Perhaps, then, ideology plays an indirect role, through the process of getting women into parliament, but it does not appear to play a direct role in recruitment of women to cabinet office. Following Norris and Lovenduski (1992), this finding suggests that "supply" rather than "demand" factors explain the greater female cabinet representation from the left than from the right.

Here again, though, I find indications of the operation of coalitional norms that affect the appointment of women. In addition to including a variable in the model to capture a political party's left/right position, the model included a variable for the coalition's left/right position. This variable was a significant predictor of the dependent variable. Even more important than a given party's ideological persuasion is the overall complexion of the government. The relationship is one of expected direction, with coalitions of parties of the left or center-left being somewhat more likely to include women than coalitions of the right or center-right.

Although the evidence about the complexion of government suggests that it is not yet time to retire the left/right hypothesis, the effect of ideology, after controlling for the mediating factor of parliamentary representation, is small.

Further, the overall strength of this relationship, in light of earlier findings, suggests that we continue to reexamine the relationship. There is evidence for convergence of behavior among parties of all ideological hues, suggesting that ideology may become an even less reliable indicator of gender inclusiveness as time passes.

Party Size

Playing a more significant role than party ideology and almost as significant a role as the coalition's ideological placement is the size of the parliamentary party. I do indeed find that, as participants in coalitions, smaller parties are more likely than larger ones to offer women opportunities to enter the government. Because this pattern holds, even when controlling for their eligibility pool compositions, it appears that smaller parties are more likely to promote women in an effort to be more electorally competitive.

Political Culture and Recruitment Norms

This analysis supports the findings of previous analysis in that, whether a cabinet system is generalist or specialist in nature, the recruitment norms affect the chances of women reaching office. Even taking into account the role of the party and of ideology, the rules of the game remain a significant predictor of whether or not women reach office.

In the case of the exceptional representation levels of women in Scandinavia, the Nordic dummy variable is significant in this latest analysis. Why would the Nordic variable obtain statistical significance in this analysis and not the one in the previous chapter? The most plausible explanation appears to concern the operationalization of political culture here employed. As discussed in the prior chapter, there is no satisfactory measure of political culture for each of the fifteen countries in this study. For this reason, political culture here has simply been operationalized in dummy fashion, assigning 1 to all Nordic countries and 0 to all non-Nordic countries. Political culture is, therefore, operationalized as a residual. The noted effect of this residual measure in this multivariate model may be attributed to culture. On the other hand, it may be attributed to some of the factors suggested here to explain the explanatory power of the measure of women of all parties in the parliament—namely, interparty competition or intraparliamentary dynamics. In other words, if we employed measures of party system competitiveness or of intraparliamentary dynamics, whose influence the findings suggest, the residual measure used here as a proxy for culture might be of less significance in the model. Clearly, future analyses should incorporate a refined measure of political culture, but they should also include the suggested measures of the competition and of intraparliamentary dynamics. Only by reanalyzing the model with some refined measures can the causal effect of political culture be properly assessed. The significance of the culture measure in this model should be viewed then as suspect, especially in light of the chapter 4 findings.

Time and Affirmative Action

Many of the lagged indicators of women's presence in parliament—from the government, from the parliament, from the party—are negatively associated with women's recruitment to cabinet rank. This means that women are being promoted either at rates faster than suggested by their presence in the parliamentary pools of eligibles or at rates slower than those suggested. The first interpretation suggests affirmative action, positive action, or positive discrimination. The second interpretation suggests simply discrimination.

One study has found that women are disadvantaged in the process of recruitment from MP to minister (MacDonald 1989). Others, in contrast, have noted the adoption of positive discrimination measures among many political parties, which would suggest the first interpretation. It is possible that in some countries women's promotion rates still lag behind men's while in other countries women are being advanced at faster rates than their presence in the pool of eligibles would suggest. It is possible, then, that these explanations are not mutually inconsistent, but that the first explanation holds in some parts of Europe and the second in others.

Change over Time

Because the findings for the earlier simple analysis of Pearson correlation coefficients revealed such contrasting patterns when the data were disaggregated by time, I repeated the analysis on two subsets of cases, first for the first seven years of the study (1968–75) and then for the last seven years (1985–92). This approach allows women's success in accessing governmental positions at the beginning of the second wave to be compared with their success in the most recent years (tables 13 and 14). Some interesting differences are apparent, both between the two subsets of cases and between each of them and the aggregate analysis.

First of all, the model's explanatory power is much greater for the late 1980s than for the early 1970s. Most of the variables in the model are designed to measure the factors that are thought to affect whether any person—male or female—enters the cabinet. The finding that these variables are much more powerful for the late 1980s than fifteen or so years earlier is very heartening for those interested in the advancement of women. It suggests that women are beginning to be recruited on terms similar to those of men.

Further evidence for the movement across time toward gender-blind re-

Table 13. Predictors of the Recruitment of Women, 1968–1975

	B	Beta
Left/Right Position		
Government/Coalition**	.18	.23
Party	.04	.04
Government Characteristics		
Type of Government	−.05	−.06
Coalition	−.06	−.03
Female MPs: Government/Coalition		
Lag 1*	−.03	−.29
Lag 2	−.03	−.20
Lag 3	.01	.10
Female MPs: Parliament		
Lag 1*	.08	.49
Lag 2	−.06	−.31
Female MPs: Party		
Current Representation**	.04	.27
Lag 1	.00	.00
Lag 2	.01	.02
Lag 3	.01	.02
Party Size/Strength		
Total Party Representation in Gov't.	.01	.09
Party's Vote Share	−.01	−.04
Timing		
Year	−.02	−.03
Change in Government	.03	.01
System Characteristics		
Nordic Dummy***	.75	.23
Generalist/Specialist***	−.02	−.23

Adjusted R^2 = .39 $F = 9.01$
$N = 244$ Sig $F = .00$

* = Significant at the .10 level
** = Significant at the .05 level
*** = Significant at the .01 level

cruitment patterns is the function of the control variable for a party's representation in government. We would expect that the more posts in government a party holds, the greater its numbers of women in government. In the 1968–75 subset of cases, this variable does not have the expected relationship. For that period, the number of posts a party held is insignificant in determining the number filled by women of the party. In later years, however, this variable has the expected relationship. The greater a party's share of the government, the greater the number of women occupying the party's share of seats. This correspondence also suggests that in recent times women are being recruited in ways that are more similar to recruitment of men.

Beyond these similarities in the earlier and later time periods, some interesting differences exist. The central finding of the earlier analysis—that it is

Table 14. Predictors of the Recruitment of Women, 1985–1992

	B	Beta
Left/Right Position		
Government/Coalition	.05	.04
Party*	.18	.08
Government Characteristics		
Type of Government***	.18	.13
Coalition	.00	.03
Female MPs: Government/Coalition		
Lag 1	−.02	−.15
Lag 2	−.02	−.11
Lag 3	−.02	−.10
Female MPs: Parliament		
Lag 1	−.01	−.04
Lag 2	.00	.02
Female MPs: Party		
Current Representation***	.04	.28
Lag 1	−.00	−.01
Lag 2	.01	.07
Lag 3	$1.20\ E{-}04$	$5.62\ E{-}04$
Party Size/Strength		
Total Party Representation in Gov't.***	.04	.21
Party's Vote Share	.00	.01
Timing		
Year	.05	.06
Change in Government	.09	.13
System Characteristics		
Nordic Dummy***	1.17	.27
Generalist/Specialist***	−.02	−.20

Adjusted R^2 = .63 F = 30.88
N = 334   Sig F = .00

* = Significant at the .10 level
** = Significant at the .05 level
*** = Significant at the .01 level

women's overall presence in the parliament as much as their presence in a parliamentary party that influences recruitment to government—is replicated.

In the most recent time period, none of the measures of women's participation in the pool of eligibles are statistically significant except women's current representation in the parliamentary party. The finding that current participation is influential whereas lagged participation is not is unexpected, based on what is known about the need for both men and women to acquire parliamentary experience before entering the government. Why would women's current representation in the parliamentary party affect that party's rates of promotion of women? The only reason I can suggest is consistent with earlier findings concerning parties' sensitivity to the institutional context: perhaps parties are responding to the prevailing institutional context. Parties are recruiting women not necessarily because their prior history (as evident in prior numbers of women MPs) suggests that their members include experienced political women ready to assume ministerial leadership, but because they are cognizant of the growing presence of significant numbers of female MPs and of the demands of gender equity (Lovenduski 1993). Further, it appears that they are also aware of rival parties' strategies intended to respond to demands for gender inclusivity.

Another interesting difference between the analysis of these subsets of cases and the earlier aggregate analysis concerns ideology. In the subset of 1985–92 cases, the influence of the ideology of the government washes out while the party's left/right placement becomes significant. Caution in interpreting this finding is in order as the magnitude of the Beta for the relationship between party ideology and women in government is quite small. Nonetheless, the finding is contrary to expectations. Both from my earlier analysis, which found that political parties of the right had at least caught up in promoting women, and from the observations of others, I had expected the ideology of the party to matter more in the earlier subset of cases and less in the latter. The reverse finding is surprising.

Conclusions

This analysis has examined the position of political parties of the left, historically the strongest promoters of women, in light of recent evidence that suggests that political parties of the right have closed—or at least narrowed—the gap. The findings of this analysis are surprising on many counts. First, prior research on the appointment of cabinet ministers has suggested that ministers are drawn predominantly from among the ranks of parliamentarians. In general, ministers are promoted up the ranks of parliamentary parties or caucuses. For women, however, the promotional ladder is not so clear. Serving in a political group is insufficient qualification for recruitment to higher office. Political parties are responsive not only to their own delegations but also to those of other parties within the system. This conclusion has been foreshadowed by the idiosyncratic accounts of others. In the United Kingdom, for example, Lovenduski and Randall (1993) note that it was initially the Social Democrats (later in conjunction with the Liberals), in search of new constituencies, that offered women opportunities for advancement within the party in the form of positive action measures. The Social Democrats' equal opportunity measures touched off a process of "competitive bidding for women's votes" to which Labour felt forced to respond.

It seems clear that political parties are likely to appoint women to the government only when their opponents are also likely to do so. Although further research is in order to clarify the reasons, prior research on the ways that a critical mass can shape an institutional environment provides some insight into factors that may be at work in addition to party competition. Dahlerup (1988, 284) maintains that the presence of a greater number of women in parliament might change the political climate of the institution in the following ways:

- changes in the perception of female politicians;
- changes in the performance and efficiency of female politicians;
- changes in the institutional culture;
- changes in the content of policy discussion and decisions; and
- increases in the power of female politicians.

It may be that party elite are more aware of and receptive to the participation of their female delegates when the institutional climate is such that it is more commonplace for women to be participants.

A subject of long debate is the question of whether women have common interests. The research presented here suggests that, inasmuch as women of all political stripes would like to see their numbers and power increase, the women of one party delegation have an interest in promoting the position of women in another. It is in the interest of social democratic women, for example, to see the conservative party's female representation increase.

Parliament intervenes in the party-to-government link for women in some ways whereas the politics of coalitional formation intervene in others. This study found surprisingly small connections between a party's left/right placement and the promotion of women. However, the ideological complexion of the coalition was found to be a factor in women's appointment to the cabinet in the earlier time period (1968–75). In those years, a party was more likely to promote women when it was participating in coalitions of the left than in coalitions of the right or center-right. This relationship existed even in the presence of controls for a party's own ideology. It suggests that political parties may be sensitive to the norms of their coalition partners and are unlikely to appoint women unless their partners are likely to do so.

Women are increasingly being promoted to the ranks of government ministers. Where this is occurring, though, it is not the result of individual parties' conscious recruitment of women, but of changes in the parliamentary institutional setting itself as more and more women are elected.

An election is coming. Universal peace is declared, and the foxes have a sincere interest in
prolonging the lives of the poultry.
George Eliot

6

The Electoral Cycle of Appointments

In further examining the circumstances under which women are appointed to
the cabinet, I sought to determine whether women are more likely to be appointed at some times than at others. Of the 449 government formations or
reshuffles during 1968–92, women were appointed in only a little more than
40 percent ($N = 181$).

Focusing on Supreme Court and cabinet appointments in the United States,
Martin (1989, 1991) has suggested the influence of electoral cycle on appointments. She argues that processes at work in the selection of appointees immediately following an election are different from those during a president's
midterm. The result is that appointments are more likely to be representative
at some times than at others. Specifically, Martin finds that a president is more
likely to appoint women to office immediately following an election and less
likely to do so during the middle of his or her administration.

Martin suggests that there is greater media attention on the appointment
process in the immediate postelection period than during midterm, pressuring the administration to make choices that are more representative of the
population as a whole. She suggests that the "symbolic importance" of female
appointments is more likely to be greater at this time (1989, 165). The political currency to be earned from descriptively representative appointments is
greater when the nation's attention is focused on the process.

During the middle of each administration, when the pressure to be representative is less, presidents rely on the so-called old boys' network, on the suggestions of close personal advisors. Limited female membership within these
advisory circles and limited female connections to these networks may result
in fewer names of women occurring among the lists of possible appointees
(Martin 1989, 1991).

The expectation that a prime minister would be under the same cycle of
temporal pressures in making appointments is consistent with what is known

about cabinet government. There are many similarities in the sources of power of prime ministers and of presidents, for example, the power to persuade (Weller 1985, 1987; Rose 1987). Both face electoral considerations and constraints.

By way of example, Alderman and Cross (1981, 1985, 1986, 1987) have detailed the many electoral considerations of prime ministers in creating and reorganizing their cabinets in the United Kingdom. Alderman and Cross find that appointments follow a parliamentary and electoral timetable such that the overwhelming majority (67 percent) of all midterm reshuffles happen during the summer parliamentary recess. The next most frequent times for cabinet reorganizations are immediately following and immediately preceding an election. The preelection reshuffles, Alderman and Cross argue, are designed to give the governing party the strongest available team of ministers with which to contend elections. They argue that the prime minister must at this time balance the need to "freshen the government's image" by bringing in youth and new ideas against the need to position experienced and trusted ministers prominently, demonstrating the governing party's competence.

Similar types of electoral pressures are faced by U.S. presidents and Western European prime ministers; for both sets of leaders, there are at least some electoral advantages to inclusiveness (Welch and Studlar 1986; Wilcox 1991); and there are similarities on both sides of the Atlantic in the patterns of public attention to the process of government formation. Given these similarities, we can reasonably extend Martin's reasoning to the political systems examined here. We might, therefore, expect a similar electoral cycle in the appointment of female cabinet members such that women would be more likely to be appointed immediately following an election. We might also extend that expectation to new regimes, even if they do not follow an election. In parliamentary democracies, governments often collapse and are replaced without reference to the public, that is, without election. Because Martin argues that it is not the election itself, but the establishment of a new regime, this extension follows naturally from her reasoning.

Further, because of Alderman and Cross's description of prime ministers' electoral considerations in the process of reshuffles, we might add an additional twist to Martin's suggestions: an expectation that governments would be more likely to appoint women immediately prior to an election. Bringing women into government during preelection maneuvers might, in Alderman and Cross's words, "freshen the government's image." Women are still political outsiders in many cases—though certainly not in all. Moreover, there is a great deal of evidence to suggest that the appointment of women would be advantageous electorally. Using Euro-barometer data from 1975, 1983, and 1987, Wilcox (1991) finds a general consensus among the publics of the European Community in support of equality of opportunity for women in the public sphere. Men and women throughout Europe have been shown to have high degrees of confidence in female legislators.[1]

Along Martin's (1989, 1991) reasoning, I expect not only an electoral cycle in the process of appointment but also a relationship between this cycle and the amount of media attention to the appointment process such that greater media coverage will result in a greater likelihood of women being appointed. The less attention the appointment process attracts, the more likely that women will not receive portfolios.

Data and Methods

For this analysis, a variable was created to capture the degree of attention directed toward the process of appointment (see appendix 3). For each cabinet reorganization from 1980 to the present, this study counted the number of news articles covering the government changes that were carried over the Reuters or United Press International wire services.[2]

The wire services reports (carried by NEXIS/LEXIS) were used for practical as well as methodological reasons. Using the wire services rather than following other media provided one uniform source of information for all fifteen countries, since the wire services both contribute to and pick up articles from the other media in each country. Further, many have shown that the news media tend to follow one another (Rose 1987).

All cases of the fate of women in appointments that precede an election are classified dichotomously, as either a "preelection maneuver" or "other." Preelection maneuvers are those series of appointments that took place twelve months or less prior to an election. The decision to use a preelection time frame of twelve months or less (rather than, for example, six months or less) is somewhat arbitrary. Nonetheless, these are the cases that are frequently viewed by the media and others as preelection maneuvers. The resultant schema classifies about one-quarter (25.6 percent) of the cases as preelection maneuvers and the rest as "other."

(Some may object that it is invalid to discuss cabinet reorganizations as preelectoral if election dates have not yet been set. I argue, however, that this classification is defensible because prime ministers are aware of the need to set election dates, and may even have dates in mind, long before the public announcement of an election date.)

In examining preelection maneuvers, I find that women are no more likely to be appointed immediately prior to an election than at any other time in the life of a government. In examining the flip side, the fate of women in postelection appointments, again I divide the cases dichotomously. This time, all cases that were the first government appointments following an election are classified as "postelection appointments." The remainder are classified as "other."

Table 15. Preelection Maneuvers and Women in Government

	Pearson Correlation
At Least One Woman Appointed	−.0976
New Members (Male and Female)	−.1426
Female New Members	−.0989
N = 442	

All correlations significant at the .05 level.

Note that in neither case was it necessary to distinguish among midterm reshuffles, as Alderman and Cross did in finding that the most frequent time of mid-term reshuffles was the summer recess. There is no theoretical reason to believe that reshuffles that occur during the summer recess are any different in nature from other midterm reshuffles or that they receive any less public attention. Accordingly, the analysis here groups together all reshuffles—summer and otherwise.

There is a strong relationship between the likelihood of a woman's appointment to a cabinet position and the time when the appointment is made. But not all is as had been expected.

Preelection Maneuvers

The expectation that governments will "freshen their image" by bringing women in is not supported. A look at Pearson correlation coefficients for the relationship between the appointment of women and preelection maneuvers reveals a negative relationship. In other words, women are less likely to be appointed in preelection maneuvers than at other times. Although this relationship is not strong ($r = -.10$), it is still statistically significant ($p = .04$). (See table 15.) The negative relationship is most likely a function of women's status as political outsiders. The Pearson correlation coefficients for the relationship between the number of new members and preelection maneuvers is negative and significant ($r = -.14$, $p = .00$). It appears, then, that governments are unlikely to bring in any new members, male or female, in preelection maneuvers.

Alderman and Cross have argued that there is a tension in the appointment process during preelection reshuffles. Prime ministers must be able to demonstrate to the publics, on the one hand, their teams of experts are capable of governing. On the other hand, prime ministers need also to demonstrate that there is fresh blood on their teams. The preelection maneuvers arguably must bring in some new members, but they must also position prominently those with experience, in whom the public has faith. My finding of a negative rela-

Table 16. Postelection Appointments in Western Europe, 1968–1992

Was a Woman Appointed?	Did Appointment Follow an Election or Government Collapse?[a]	
Column %	No	Yes
No	81.72	31.49
Yes	18.28	68.51
Total	100.00	100.00

$X^2 = 115$
$DF = 1$
$N = 449$

[a]No = appointments were part of a midterm reshuffle.

tionship between new members and preelection maneuvers suggests, contrary to Alderman and Cross, that the tension between appointing a team of experts and bringing new blood into the cabinet at preelectoral junctures is most often resolved in favor of entrusting government to those who are most experienced.

This negative relationship becomes more interesting when we note the differences between the entrance of male and female new members. The relationship between female new members and preelection maneuvers is less strongly negative ($r = -.10$, $p = .04$) than the relationship between all new members and preelection maneuvers. But the fact that the relationship between female new entrants and preelection maneuvers is not as strong as the relationship between all new entrants and preelection maneuvers suggests that when prime ministers are interested in injecting their administrations with new blood prior to an election, they are more likely to turn to women than to men. Caution should be exercised in attributing great importance to differences between male and female new entrants at this time, however, because the differences between the two are quite small.

Postelection Appointments

For those appointments following an election, the analysis supports the expectations. In other words, the likelihood that a woman will be appointed to a cabinet position is much greater in a new cabinet than in a midterm reshuffle (see table 16). In more than two-thirds of all the cases in which a woman was appointed to government, the appointment followed an election. Moreover, in 82 percent of the cases in which elections did not precede an appointment, no woman was appointed. This finding indicates that women are appointed almost exclusively in the wake of an election.

The analysis raises the question of why this relationship is so strong. What accounts for this electoral cycle of appointments? Is it, as Martin argues, that a greater degree of attention is devoted to the process of appointment, creating more pressure on political elites to make decisions that are egalitarian? Or are there other explanations for this trend?

There is in fact a strong positive relationship between the volume of news coverage devoted to government appointments and the timing of appointments ($r = .43, p = .00$). The volume of news coverage surrounding the initial formation of a government perhaps reflects greater public interest. The stakes are highest at these times, as all portfolios are up for grabs. Indeed, in some political systems where bargaining preceding government formation is protracted, the identity of the players in a new coalition may even be unclear at first. Public uncertainty about issues of both partisanship and individual leadership results in significant interest in the process at this time.

There is also a very strong relationship between incumbency and the timing of elections ($r = .64, p = .00$). It is intuitive that there would be a positive relationship. Those members of a government that is returned by a successful run in a general election are likely to be returned in postelection appointments. But every time a shift in the electoral fortunes of parties results in a different coalition, all of the seats in the government are up for grabs.

Incumbency, or the return of ministers who were members of the prior government, is measured for the purposes of this analysis by the number of new members in the government (persons who did not serve in the prior administration). The measure is thus a sort of anti-incumbency indicator. It is largest when incumbency is weakest and smallest when incumbency is greatest. Therefore, the strong, positive association of the incumbency measure means that new entrants into a cabinet (nonincumbents) are most likely to enter when a new government is formed. Might the timing of elections be related to the appointment of women because the power of incumbency, which works against women, is less significant during the postelection period than at midterm?

Many people have argued that incumbency is one of the biggest factors—if not the single biggest factor—working against the election of women (Anderson and Thorson 1984; Welch and Studlar 1987, 1992; Darcy, Welch, and Clark 1994; Young 1991; Studlar 1994; Studlar and Matland 1994; Matland 1994a, 1994b). Writing about the "year of the woman" in the United States, Clyde Wilcox (1994) notes that the unusually high number of open seats and the general anti-incumbency mood of the public were crucial factors in sending women to Congress in large numbers in 1992.[3] Some have found that once women achieve incumbency, they are just as difficult as men to dislodge from office (Welch and Studlar 1987). Perhaps the power of incumbency similarly works against women's achievement of office through the appointive route.

Table 17. Electoral Cycle of Appointments, 1968–1992

Variable	Parameter Estimate	Standard Error	Odds Ratio
Intercept	1.691	0.186	5.425
Number of New Ministers	0.100	0.027	1.106
Number of Articles	−0.001	0.008	0.999
New Government[a]	−1.444	0.313	0.236

Criteria for assessing model fit:
    −2 Log L   130.00, $DF = 3$
    Score   123.69, $DF = 3$

[a]Where 0 = Mideterm reshuffle; 1 = new government.

I am not suggesting that the power of incumbency is the same in the United states and in Western Europe or that the mechanisms through which incumbency is perpetuated are the same. Without doubt, incumbency is a more potent factor in the candidate-centered races of the United States than in the party-centered ones of Western Europe. In Western Europe, too, though, party selectorates are under pressure to reslate or readopt MPs in good standing. The British Labour Party, for example, has adopted a policy that mandates reselection of Labour MPs, thereby ensuring that those Labour MPs from safe seats will be returned in an election (Lovenduski and Randall 1993). In France, the practice of *cumul des mandats*, or simultaneous occupation of multiple offices, is one way in which a few individuals are able to monopolize positions of power for an extended period of time. For this reason, some have speculated that limiting the *cumul des mandats* might result in greater numbers of women in office (Kaplan 1992).

To further test the relationship between elections and the appointment of women, multivariate analysis using logistic regression was conducted. Logistic regression uses maximum likelihood to estimate the parameters for binary or ordinal response variables. This technique rather than Logit is most appropriate for the analysis because two of the independent variables are continuous (Cox and Snell 1989; Aldrich and Rhode 1978). The model includes the measure of news coverage of appointments; the anti-incumbency measure; the number of new ministers who received appointments; and a measure of whether the appointment was part of a midterm reshuffle or the formation of a new government. Results of the analysis are reported in table 17.[4]

From table 17, we see that the change in the log odds of there being a woman appointed to a cabinet position is

$$(1.691) + (.10 \times \text{incumbency}) + (-.001 \times \text{news coverage})$$
$$+ (-1.444 \times \text{new cabinet}).$$

In other words, for every unit change in incumbency there is a corresponding 10.52 percent increase in the chances that a woman will be appointed.[5] This is one respect in which appointments do not differ from elections. The chances that a woman will access office are tied very significantly to the degree to which incumbents retain a hold on power. If the power of incumbency is less, as it often is following an election that results in a change in government, the chances that a woman will be appointed are greater.

Further, even after controlling for the degree of incumbency, the timing of appointments continues to matter. The effect is so strong that when the appointment occurs following an election or the formation of a new coalition, there is a 76.3 percent greater chance that a woman will be appointed.

Timing is a critical variable. Women are far more likely to be appointed to office following an election than during midterm and this is not solely a function of incumbency. What explains the electoral cycle of appointments?

Surprisingly, the relationship between timing and the appointment of women has nothing to do with the amount of attention devoted to the process, as measured by the volume of news coverage. The relationship between the amount of news coverage and the likelihood that a woman will be appointed is statistically insignificant. It appears that, contrary to what Martin has argued, the extent of media attention devoted to the distribution of political spoils does not play a role in pressuring political elites to be egalitarian. With that said, it is important to note the ways in which this analysis differs from Martin's. Martin argues that the media attention given the appointment process is significant only after a regime change, only when there is a new administration. My analysis does not directly distinguish between those government appointments that were made following an election that brought in a new coalition and those made following a general election that "confirmed" an existing coalition in office. Indirectly, this distinction is accounted for through the incumbency variable. Although it is unlikely that this distinction accounts for the differences in findings, caution should govern the amount of attention paid to one negative finding.

The finding that timing is such a powerful predictor of whether or not a woman is appointed is probably best understood by contrasting the performance of the first model with a second that seeks to determine to what degree these same explanatory variables are useful in predicting the number of women appointed to office. For this analysis, ordinary least squares regression was possible because no binary response variable was in operation (table 18).

Although the second model performs well, explaining just over 26 percent of the variance associated with the number of new women entering the cabinet, the only independent variable that continues to have statistical impor-

Table 18. Predictors of the Number of New Members Who Are Women

Dependent Variable: Number of new female members[a]

Variable	Parameter Estimate	Standard Error	t
Intercept	0.10	0.09	.23
Incumbency	−0.12	0.01	.00
News	−0.00	0.00	.30
New Cabinet	−0.13	0.16	.40

N = 439
R-square = .27
Adj R-sq = .26

[a]OLS Regression. See table 3 for a definition of independent variables.

tance is the variable for incumbency. Incumbency remains a strong explanatory variable negatively associated with the appointment of women. Timing of appointments, however, is no longer significant. It is a paradox that timing is a powerful factor in explaining whether or not a woman is appointed but only a weak indicator of how many women are appointed (see "Timing" section, below).

In some ways, the preceding analysis raises more questions than it answers. Why does news coverage of the appointment process seem to matter little? Why are women much more likely to be appointed following an election or formation of a new coalition? And why does the postelectoral period serve as only a weak predictor of the number of women who are appointed if it is such a powerful explanatory variable in predicting whether or not a woman is appointed?

Media Attention

There are several reasons why media attention to the appointment process might be insignificant. The first, and probably the most counterintuitive, is that governments are unaware of or unconcerned about the press coverage. This seems highly improbable, as governments go to great lengths to ensure that their press is favorable, carefully selecting spokespersons. Given government awareness of the necessity of maintaining public confidence if reelection is to be a possibility, disregard for the media would be hard to explain. A second possible explanation is that prime ministers, although aware of the attention focused on their selections for office, do not necessarily respond by appointing women. Perhaps premiers do not perceive the appointment of women to be electorally advantageous. This too is an unlikely scenario, as gender became an explicit issue for many political parties during the 1980s (Lovenduski 1993).

The most likely explanation, therefore, lies with the unequal treatment by the press of individual sectors of government. The volume of news coverage is portfolio-specific. Rose (1987) finds that the British premier and the chancellor of the exchequer receive front-page coverage in the *Times* of London at least every other day. Other portfolios that Rose finds receive a great deal of media attention include the Foreign Office, the Home Office, the Ministry of Trade and Industry, and the Ministries of Defence and the Environment (Rose 1987, 87). With the exception of Environment, these are portfolios that women across Europe hold only infrequently. The portfolios allocated to women fall disproportionately in the categories of health and welfare (see chap. 2). As long as these strong patterns of sectorization persist, female ministers are likely to receive less media attention than their male counterparts.

Analysis by Davis and Lancaster (1993) shows that the countries that have positive associations between female new cabinet ministers and media coverage—Finland, France, The Netherlands, and Norway—are some of the same countries in which women are breaking new ground, occupying positions that were formerly the exclusive domain of male politicians. In Finland, Elizabeth Rehn has been minister of defense since June 1990. In Norway, Gro Harlem Brundtland is three-time prime minister, and the women in her cabinet include the minister of agriculture, Gunhild Oeyangen; the economically powerful minister of fisheries, Oddrun Petersen; and minister of trade and shipping, Eldrid Nordboe. In France, the controversial Edith Cresson served first as minister of agriculture, then as prime minister; Edwige Avice served as secretary of state for defense (a junior portfolio) in the Fabius government. Women in The Netherlands have participated in government in sizable numbers, most frequently in those sectors traditionally open to women.

Incumbency

Without doubt, the most consistent predictor of whether or not women achieve cabinet office is incumbency. In this respect, appointments are no different from elections. Because women remain, by and large, political outsiders, the power of incumbency—which appears to be a significant force in the appointive channel just as in the elective—works against women.

No doubt, part of the reason for the strong relationship between the timing of appointments and the success of women in gaining office is that incumbency is less of a factor following an election that brings the collapse of a coalition. Perhaps one of the most interesting findings of this study is that even after controlling for the effects of incumbency, timing remains a significant predictor of the success of women in obtaining at least one portfolio in a cabinet.

Table 19. Mean Number of New Female Government Members by Country, 1968–1992

Country	Mean	Standard Deviation
Austria	0.56	1.04
Belgium	0.55	1.03
Denmark	0.88	1.11
Finland	0.89	1.37
France	0.55	1.16
Germany	0.33	0.61
Greece	0.11	0.32
Ireland	0.22	0.42
Italy	0.17	0.38
Netherlands	0.69	1.45
Norway	2.18	2.70
Portugal	0.17	0.54
Spain	0.14	0.48
Sweden	1.44	2.14
U. K.	0.14	0.47

Timing

Why is timing such a powerful predictor of the probability of a woman being appointed but not of the number of new female cabinet members? An examination of the number of women entering ministerial office in table 19 might provide some answers. Despite the inroads that women have made in some countries in the last few years, there has been very little variation in their numbers among the countries of this study. Strong patterns of tokenism persist in the vast majority of the countries. The largest mean number of new female cabinet members is 2.18 (Norway). This is a paltry maximum. In some other countries, the norm of appointing even a single woman has yet to be established (Lovenduski 1986).

There is significant demand among the public for a woman to be included among the ranks of the government officials. As discussed, public outcry accompanied the absence of a woman in both the first Major government in England and the Zolotas government in Greece. By Thatcher's own account of her political career, she frequently benefited from the tokenist maxim. She says that she got her first government position, in the Pensions ministry, when Pat Hornsby-Smith, "perhaps the star woman politician of the time" resigned (Thatcher 1995, 68). Thatcher speculates that Edward Heath's keen awareness of the need for at least one woman in his cabinet may have been behind his decision to stand by her when press headlines such as "Maggy Thatcher the Milk Snatcher," "The Most Unpopular Woman in Britain," and "The Lady Nobody Loves" were villifying her (181, 188). Of her time as a shadow minister, Thatcher writes, "I did not make a particularly important contribution to the Shadow Cabinet. Nor was I asked to do so. For Ted [Heath] and perhaps others I was principally there as the statutory woman whose main task was to explain what 'women'—Kiri Te Kanawa, Barbara Cartland, Esther Rantzen, Stella Rimington and all the rest of our uniform, undifferentiated sex—were likely to think and want on troublesome issues" (144).

Conclusion

This analysis shows that the electoral cycle of appointments is not a function of media attention but is, at least in part, a function of incumbency. Incumbency has long been known to play a role in keeping women from obtaining government office in elections. Incumbency, as this analysis shows, also plays a role in the process of appointments.

Even after controlling for incumbency, though, timing remains a critical explanatory factor. Women are 76.1 percent more likely to be appointed immediately following an election than they are in midterm rehuffles. An explanation for this pattern is brought into relief when the power of timing as an explanatory variable is compared in the two models presented here.

Because virtually every government wants to appoint at least one woman to office, timing is a very strong predictor of the probability that a woman will be appointed. Once a new government has satisfied the norm of one woman in office, however, there is less cause to appoint a woman during midterm reorganizations. This constraint reflects abiding patterns of tokenism, the idea that "one is enough" (Matland 1994, 12).

7

Conclusion:
A Discussion of Appointments and Elections

President Bill Clinton's laborious efforts to ensure that his administration "looks like" America received a great deal of media attention because the notion that government appointments should mirror the society from which they are drawn was considered so extraordinary. Government appointments have not ever looked like America—or any other citizenry, for that matter. Of 5,965 cabinet-level appointments made in Western Europe over the last twenty-five years, only 586, or 9.8 percent, went to women. Why do political appointments not mirror more closely the societies from which they are drawn?

The works of Darcy, Welch, and Clark (1994), Rule (1989), Moncrief and Thompson (1992), and others have helped us understand the reasons why elections tend to produce officials who are not descriptively representative. Indeed, political scientists have amassed a great deal of knowledge about elections. Yet some of the most powerful positions in the democratic world are not elective but appointive in nature. These include seats on the U.S. Supreme Court, the office of U.S. attorney general, ambassadorships, and the powerful heads of ministries in parliamentary cabinets. This project has attempted to extend the literature on women and politics beyond the discussion of women and elections by focusing on the dynamics of the appointment process. By examining the ministerial appointments of women in Western Europe, this work has attempted to identify factors specific to the process of appointment that contribute to making political power descriptively representative in terms of gender.

Yet in discussing appointments, I have repeatedly returned to examining elections, which influence and constrain appointments in a variety of ways. First, I find an electoral cycle to the appointment of women. The very act of holding elections increases the likelihood that a woman will be appointed by more than 76 percent. Women are much more likely to be appointed following an election than they are during midterm reshuffles.

The greater likelihood of women being appointed following an election is in part a function of incumbency. Incumbency, one of the factors significantly constraining the participation of women in electoral arenas, is also an obstacle to the participation of women in appointive office. For every vacancy that exists in the cabinet, the chances of a woman's being appointed increase by almost 11 percent. The fact that governments are more permeable to all participants following an election is part of the explanation for women more frequently receiving appointments following an election than during midterm reshuffles or preelection maneuvers.

Focusing on preelection maneuvers, those reshuffles of the cabinet designed to give the governing party or parties the greatest competitive advantage in the electoral home stretch, also highlights the importance of incumbency as a constraint on women's access to high office. Both women and men external to the government are less likely to be appointed in preelection maneuvers. Preelection maneuvers are generally characterized by a reallocation of responsibilities among the government notables tested at the ministerial level rather than by the incorporation of new talent from among the parliamentary ranks. However, when new persons do enter the cabinet during these preelection maneuvers, they are more likely to be female than male. While incumbency disadvantages all persons—and may disadvantage women more than men in the process of elections—at certain times in the cycle of government formation and termination, at least, incumbency may disadvantage men more significantly than it encumbers women.

The electoral cycle of female appointments is not the result of media scrutiny of the appointive process, as some have suggested. Although there is heightened media scrutiny of the appointment process in the wake of elections, it is not significantly associated with the appointment of women. Media attention tends to hone in on two types of issues or events surrounding appointments: on scandal and on those portfolios that are deemed by many to be the most powerful or most prestigious—portfolios such as the Ministries of Finance, Defense, and Trade. As repeatedly stated here, there is gender segregation such that women tend to receive appointments in a narrow range of government responsibilities, almost all of which fall outside the public eye. By these standards, the appointment of women is often less newsworthy than the appointment of many of their male counterparts.[1]

It is suggested here that the currently observed pattern of association between elections and the appointment of women—although likely to persist well into the future—may not be a permanent feature. In those countries where women have begun to win portfolios outside the traditionally female domain, Norway and Sweden for example, the relationship between the appointment of women and the occurrence of an election does not hold. In fact, the appointment of women in these countries is slightly more likely during midterm reshuffles than following an election (see Davis and Lancaster, 1993). This fact, in combination with the lack of statistical relationship between the timing of elections and the number of female appointments, suggests that the relationship between the appointment of women and elections is a function of persistent patterns of tokenism. Even if media attention is not a factor in the appointment of women, governments seem to behave as if it were. In this regard, Janet Martin's (1989) study is right on the mark in suggesting that timing matters in the appointment of women because of the greater "symbolic importance" of their appointment following elections.

The suggestion here that this relationship may not endure indefinitely, despite the lack of consistent unidirectional advances in the representation of women in all fifteen countries of this study, is based on the significant changes in the representation of women in many of the countries. In almost all fifteen countries, women are significantly better represented in the 1990s than they were in the 1960s. But a continuation of this change should not be taken for granted. The percentage of women holding parliamentary seats in Sweden actually declined following the 1991 elections, for the first time since 1936. Bystydzienski (1988), Faludi (1991), and others have described the backlash against women that often follows their acceptance of new roles, including participation in formal political arenas.

Among other ways in which elections and appointments are intertwined, elections are significant in determining the pool of eligibles from which ministers are drawn. Further, the rules of the game for the recruitment of ministers are such that some form of apprenticeship in parliament is generally a requirement. The appointment of women to office is also tied, therefore, to their history of achievement of electoral office.

More than two-thirds of all ministers in this study are recruited from their national parliaments. The rules of ministerial recruitment are such that some systems, generalist systems, recruit almost exclusively from among the ranks of parliamentarians and require lengthy parliamentary tenure before promotion to ministerial office. Other systems—the more specialist systems—are more permeable, recruit a number of nonparliamentarians, and exhibit shorter periods of parliamentary training before certification as eligible for higher office.[2]

The difference between generalist and specialist systems in terms of recruitment patterns is rooted in different conceptions of ministerial office. Systems falling close to the generalist pole emphasize the representative function of ministerial office, whereas systems closer to the specialist pole emphasize an administrative function alongside the representative one. Further, the emphasis on representation over administration in generalist systems results in the reward of specific skills, such as prowess in parliamentary debate, that are not necessarily related to capacity to administer effectively.

The difference between the two types of systems is significant not only for initial appointment to ministerial office but also for the direction of ministerial careers subsequent to appointment. In generalist systems, mobility within the cabinet, or promotion, usually entails moving from one ministerial area to another. Among generalists, there is a clearer recognition that not all ministries are equal. It is thought that a minister's competence in one functional area will readily translate into competence in another. In specialist systems, on the other hand, a greater degree of functional specialization is the norm, and movement within (as from junior to senior minister) rather than between ministries is not uncommon (Larsson 1988).

This study shows that the two recruitment patterns are not gender neutral. The rules of the game matter. Women are much more likely to receive appointments in the more permeable specialist-type systems than in the generalist type. The fact that women have lower levels of participation in the cabinets of generalist-type systems is in part a result of the greater time period between election and appointment in generalist systems. Women appointees will thus have served in the national parliaments of these systems longer than in specialist systems.

Women in the national parliaments are more common in countries where the system is specialist rather than generalist. This difference raises a number of questions that are beyond the scope of this study. Is the conception of political office that has given rise to more permeable recruitment patterns rooted in a specific type of political culture? Or, perhaps, does the emphasis on technical skill, rather than some less objective conception of office such as "representational capacity," enhance women's chances for obtaining office for reasons outlined in chapter 3 (namely, having many of the same qualifications as men)? Further, does the difference in permeability of office have an interaction or feedback effect on the motivation of women to seek office such that women in more generalist systems are dissuaded from seeking parliamentary office whereas women in specialist-type systems are encouraged?

Time and the necessity of having completed a parliamentary stint are not the only factors at work in differentiating these two types of systems. Even when this study controls for the numbers of women in parliament—greater in specialist-type systems—it finds that women are disadvantaged in generalist systems. Women hold appointive office in generalist systems in numbers lower than expected given their parliamentary presence—even given the longer time lags.

This finding may be related in part to the sectorization of female MPs within parliaments. Despite their increasing service in leadership posts and the beginnings of participation in nontraditional committee areas, female parliamentarians' committee representation is still highly concentrated in traditional areas.

Perhaps the most surprising finding of this study is that women's parliamentary participation translates into governmental participation in unanticipated ways. The conventional wisdom about cabinet ministers is that political parties have considerable autonomy in selecting from among their respective pool of eligibles—their parliamentary delegations. Yet Multivariate analysis shows that the presence of women in a party's parliamentary party is not the best predictor of women's appointment to cabinet office. Rather, it is the size of the female contingency in the parliament as a whole that is the best predictor of whether women are recruited. Political parties are most likely to appoint women to office when other parties within their system are also likely to do so.

Although a definitive explanation for this finding is beyond the scope of this work, at least two explanations are possible. First, political parties may be responding to the perception of within-system competition for the female electorate. A competitive party system alone is clearly insufficient to promote women (as in Greece's highly competitive system, in which women are rarely appointed to the highest offices). Once women have made inroads into one party or group of parties within a system, other parties may feel the necessity of responding similarly by promoting women. Scholars of the Norwegian system have noted that once the Social Democratic Party implemented positive discrimination measures in favor of women, all other parties except one in the system soon followed with their own versions of affirmative action or positive discrimination (Bystydzienski 1988, 1992).

The preceding discussion of political parties' promotion of women assumes that parties are in some way external to women or that women are somehow passive recipients of political parties' decisions to tolerate or promote inclusiveness. An alternative scenario, consistent with the party competition hypothesis, is that as women achieve office via one party's recruitment channels, they may acquire the resources or the motivation to succeed in other channels.

In addition to the possibility that within-system competition among political parties is the reason why women's overall level of representation in parliament is such a powerful predictor of women's chances of recruitment, a second possible explanation is the presence or absence of a critical mass of female parliamentarians. Further, these two hypotheses need not be mutually exclusive. It is possible that the presence or absence of a critical mass and the

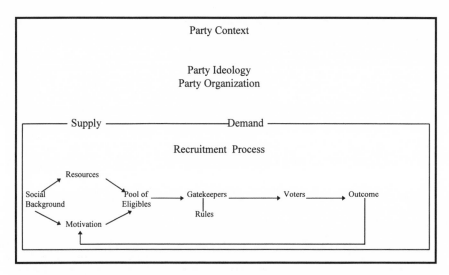

Figure 10. Electoral Recruitment of Women

Source: Joni Lovenduski and Pippa Norris, eds. *Gender and Party Politics* (London: Sage, 1993), 311. Reprinted with permission. Note that Norris places this recruitment process within the context of the political system, including the political culture, electoral system, party system, and party competition.

competitiveness of the party system are factors that interact in affecting the likelihood of recruitment of women. In other words, a highly competitive party system in which there is not a critical mass of female parliamentarians might not result in greater numbers of women being recruited, whereas a competitive system with a critical mass of female parliamentarians would do so.

While this analysis does not definitively explain the relationship between parliamentary participation and the appointment of women to cabinet positions, it does offer some insight. Clearly, the rules of the game—that is, the norms of recruitment—are not gender neutral. There is also a significant amount of evidence that political parties are very sensitive to the presence or absence of women in the parliament. This sensitivity may mean that parties are more responsive to the parliamentary environment than to their own female constituencies. Alternatively, it may mean that women have greater resources within their parliamentary parties—for whatever reasons—when parliament includes significant numbers of women from other party groups as well.

Norris (1993, 311) posits a systems model of the election of women that makes similar arguments about the electoral process. In Norris's model, the supply of candidates is influenced by election outcomes, that is, by the success of women in obtaining elective office (fig.10).

Because of the connections noted here between elections and appoint-

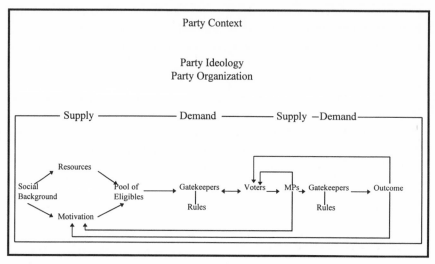

Figure 11. Elections and Appointments: A Model of Recruitment

ments, an extension of Norris's model to the process of appointments seems logical. I posit that Norris's outcome, that is, persons elected to the parliament, becomes the pool of eligibles (members of parliament), who are similarly judged by elite gatekeepers and affected by the rules of the parliamentary game. The outcome is appointments to the cabinet (fig.11).

In addition to Norris's suggestion of a feedback loop that connects the election outcome with the motivation of potential eligibles, I also posit that the outcome affects voters' perception of candidates (hence, double feedback loops). A feedback loop between election outcome and candidate evaluation by voters has been suggested elsewhere (Wilcox 1991). Wilcox suggests that Westerners find difficulty in maintaining that women are incapable of serving competently in public office in the face of empirical evidence to the contrary.

The appointment of women to cabinet positions can thus be seen as a two-stage process: election to parliament followed by appointment to government. The model of the process presented here is—like all models—a simplification of reality.

From this analysis of the appointment of women to cabinet positions in Western Europe, we can generalize to the appointment of women in other arenas as well. First, it seems clear that membership in the pool of eligibles alone does not result in appointment. In other words, even when women parliamentarians participate in the pool of eligibles from which the party recruits, they are not assured of being appointed. The findings here suggest that in making such appointments, elite gatekeepers have a heightened sensitivity to the desirability of inclusiveness. Heightened sensitivity may result from the perception of intense scrutiny (such as after an election). Alternately, it may come from the transformation of the political environment by the presence of a critical mass. Gatekeepers' responsiveness to their female eligibles may increase if the presence of a critical mass presents female politicians with additional resources (defined broadly).

Further, as long as the principal organizing agent of liberal democracies is the political party, it is impossible to rule out the motivation of vote maximization. If there is a perception that other parties within the system are behaving (or are likely to behave) in ways that will secure additional votes, we can expect a Downsian sort of accommodation or alteration in policy so as to remain competitive.

Appendix 1: Variables and Coding

Dependent Variables

recruitment norms (chap. 4): number of women in government

party-parliament nexus (chap. 5): number of women from party in government

electoral cycle (chap. 6): appointment/nonappointment of women

    0 = no women appointed

    1 = at least one woman appointed

Independent Variables

change in government

    1 = new government (government formation following an election or the change of prime ministers)

    0 = reshuffle or replacement of single minister

coalition

    1 = coalition

    0 = single-party government

Defense committee participation = percentage of seats on defense committee of respective national parliament (lower house if bicameral) as given by the IPU and reported in table 2.

female new members of government = nonincumbent females

generalist/specialist

    Those countries closest to the generalist end of the continuum have high scores on this continuum; specialist countries have lower values. (Individual country values are reported in table 6.)

government/coalition's left/right position

    1 = right-wing dominance (share of seats in government 66.6 percent or greater)

2 = right-center complexion (share of seats of right and center parties in government between 33.3 and 66.6 percent each)

3 = balanced (share of center larger than 50 percent)

4 = left-center complexion (share of seats of left and center parties in government between 33.3 and 66.6 percent each)

5 = left-wing dominance (share of seats of left in government larger than 66.6 percent)

incumbency (reverse) = number of persons entering the government who were not part of the prior administration

Nordic/Scandinavian dummy variable (also referred to as the political culture variable).

0 = country outside Scandinavia

1 = Scandinavian country (Denmark, Norway, Finland, Sweden)

news = number of news articles covering the current government appointments

parties (number of parties in coalition)

party's left/right position

1 = right

2 = center

3 = left

Austria

Socialist Party (SPÖ)	Left
People's Party (ÖVP)	Center
Freedom Party (FPÖ)	Right

Belgium

Flemish Christian Socialist (CVP)	Center
French-speaking liberal (PRL)	Right
French-speaking Christian (PSC)	Right
Flemish-speaking liberal (PVV)	Right
French-speaking liberal (PS)—split with PSC	Left
Dutch-speaking socialist (BSP)	Left
Parti Socialiste Belge (PSB)	Left
Free Democrats–Belgium (FDF)	Center
Volksunie Flemish Nationalist	Right
Rassemblement Walloon (RW)	Left
Liberal Walloonian Party (PRLW)	Right
Liberals–Parti de la Liberté du progrès (PLP; precursor to PRL)	Right

Denmark

Social Democrats (SD)	Center
Liberal Democrats (LD)	Left
Conservatives (KF)	Right
Center Democrats (CD)	Center
Christian People's Party (KRF)	Center
Radical Liberal	Left

Finland

Liberals (LKP)	Center
Swedish People's Party (SPP or SFP)	Center
Rural Party (SMP)	Center
Social Democrats (SDP)	Left
Centre Party (KESK)	Center
Conservative (National Coalition) (KOK)	Right
Finnish People's Dem. League (SKDL)	Left
Finnish People's Dem. League and the Communist Party of Finland (SKDL /SKP)	Left
Finnish Christian Union (SKL)	Left

France

Socialist (PS)	Left
Left Radical Movement (MRG)	Center
UDF-Radical	Center
Union for French Democracy (UDF)	Center
(UDF-CDS)	Center
UDF-Center of Social Democrats	Center
Gaullist–Rally for the Republic (RPR)	Right
UDF-Republican (UDF-PR)	Center
UDF-Social Democrat (UDF-PSD)	Right
Communist (PCF)	Left
Unified Socialists (PSU)	Left
Democrats	Center
Gistaing Majority	Right
National Center of Independents and Peasants (UDF-CNIP)	Right
Union des démocrates pour la République (UDR) (Gaullist)	Right
Democratic Progress Party (PDM)	Right
Ind. Republican	Right

Centre Democrat	Right
Radical	Right
Reformateur	Right
CDS (created May 1976: merger of CDS and Centre Democrat parties)	Center
MSL (associated with UDR in Barre government)	Right
UFE (Union pour la France en Europe)	Right

Germany

Free Democratic Party (FDP)	Center
Social Democratic Party (SPD)	Left
Christian Democratic Party (CDU/CSU)	Right
Christian Social Union (Bavaria) (CSU)	Right
German Social Union (DSU)	Right

Greece

National Radical Union (NRU)	Right
Centre Union (CU)	Left
New Democracy (ND)	Right
Pan-Hellenic Social Movement (PASOK)	Left

Ireland

Fine Gael (FG)	Right
Fianna Fail (FF)	Right
Labour (LAB)	Left
Progressive Democrats (PD)	Left

Italy

Christian Democrat (CD)	Center
Socialist (PSI) (later PSU)	Left
Republican (PRI)	Center
Unitarian Socialists (PSR)	Left
Social Democrats (PSDI)	Center
Liberals (PLI)	Center
Communists (PCI) (later Democratic Party of the Left)	Left

Netherlands

Labor Party (PvdA)	Left
Catholic People's Party (KVP)	Center

Liberals (Party of Freedom and Democracy) (VVD)	Right
Anti-Revolutionary Party (ARP)	Center
Christian Historical Union (CHU)	Right
Democrats-66 (D-66)	Center
Democratic Socialists (DS-70)	Left
Communist Party and State Reform Party	Left
Radical Political Party (PPR)	Left
Reformed Political Association (FPF)	Right
Pacifist Socialist Party (PSP)	Left
Farmer's Party	Right
Christian Democratic Appeal (CDA)	Center
Groen Links (alliance of four left-wing parties, not including Greens)	Left

Norway

Labour (DNA)	Left
Conservatives (H)	Right
Center Party (SP)	Center
Christian People's Party (KrF)	Center
Liberals (LP)	Left

Portugal

Açâo Nacional Popular (ANP)	Right
Socialist Party (PSP)	Left
Communist (PC)	Left
Democratic Popular Party (PPD)	Center
Portuguese Democratic Movement (MDP)	Center
Portuguese Communist Party (PCP)	Left
Social Democratic Party (PSD)	Center
Party of Democratic Social Center (CDS)	Right
Uniâo Nacional (UN)	Right
Popular Monarchist Party (PPM)	Left

Spain

National Movement	Right
Union of the Democratic Centre (UCD)	Center
Spanish Socialist Workers' Party (PSOE)	Left
Catalan wing of the PSOE (PSC)	Left

Sweden
   Social Democrats (SDP)   Left
   Liberals (Folkpartiet) (FP)   Center
   Centre Party (CP)   Center
   Communists (VPK)   Left
   Conservatives (Moderate) (M)   Right
   Christian Democrats (KDS)   Right

United Kingdom
   Conservatives   Right
   Labour   Left

party's representation in government = total number of ministers the party
   has in the current government coalition
party's vote share = share of vote in most recent parliamentary election
type of government
   1 = single-party government
   2 = minimal winning coalition
   3 = surplus coalition
   4 = single-party minority government
   5 = multiparty minority government
   6 = caretaker government
year = year of cabinet formation

Measures of Women in the Pool of Eligibles

The measures of women's presence in the pool of eligibles were constructed in such a way as to count any woman only once. Therefore, women who were members of the parliamentary party specified in the dependent variable were excluded in counting the women who were members of the government's parties. Similarly the number of women in the parliament excluded the number of women members of any party participating in the government. In other words:

women in parliament = all women in parliament – number of women from
   governmental parties
women in government = all women members of government – number of
   women from parliamentary party in question
women in parliament from the party
   current rep = number of women in current parliamentary group
   lag 1 = number of women in the parliamentary party after the previous
   election
   lag 2 = number of women in the parliamentary party two electoral periods
   prior

women in parliament from the government

    lag 1 = number of women in parliament who are also members of the government coalition's parties in the previous parliament (lag one electoral period)

    lag 2 = number of women in parliament who are also members of the government coalition's parties in two parliaments prior (lag two electoral periods)

women in parliament

    lag 1 = number of women in previous parliament (lag one electoral period)

    lag 2 = number of women in two parliaments prior (lag two electoral periods)

Appendix 2: Parties and Parliaments Providing Data

Parties

Austria
   Freedom Party
   People's Party

Belgium
   Liberal (PRL) (French-speaking)
   Christian Socialist Party (CVP) (Flemish)
   Volksunie

Denmark
   Det Radikale Venstre
   Det Konservative
   Center Democrats
   Christian People's Party (KRF)
   Venstre
   Socialdemokratiet

Finland
   Liberals (LKP)
   Kansallinen Kokoomus
   Suomen Maaseudun Puolue
   Suomen Sosialidemokraattinen Puolue (SSP)
   Svenska Folkpartiet
   Vasemmistoliitto

France
   Left Radical Movement
   Rally for the Republic (RPR)

Communist (PCF)
Mouvement des Démocrates
Union for French Democracy (UDF)

Germany
Social Democrats (SPD)
Free Democrats (FDP)
Christian Social Union (CSU)

Greece
Pasok

Italy
Italian Communist Party (PCI)
Christian Democratic Party (DC)
Social Democrats (PSDI)

Ireland
Progressive Democrats
Fine Gael

Netherlands
Labor Party (PvdA)
Reformed Political Association (FPF)
Staatkundig Gereformeerde
Groen Links
Democrats-66 (D-66)

Norway
Socialist Left Party
Labor Party (DNA)
Christian People's Party (KrF)

Portugal
Party of Democratic Social Center (CDS)
Social Democratic Party (PSD)
Communist Party (PC)

Spain
Spanish Socialist Workers' Party (PSOE)
Partido Popular (PP)

Sweden
Social Democrats (SDP)
Liberals (FP)
Moderate Samlingspartiet
Christian Democrats (KDS)
Centerpartiet
Vansterpartiet

United Kingdom
Labour
Conservative

Parliaments
Austrian National Assembly
Belgian Chamber of Representatives
Belgian Senate
Danish Folketing
Dutch Chamber of the States General
French National Assembly
Greek Chamber of Deputies
Italian Chamber of Deputies
Norwegian Storting
Portuguese Assembly
Spanish Congress of Deputies
Swedish Riksdag

Appendix 3: The NEXIS Search

Media Coverage of Government Appointments

The exact NEXIS search term for each government change was

[Prime Minister's name] w/15 cabinet or (council of ministers) or minister! or government or coalition and reorganize! or dismiss! or nominate! or appoint! or collapse! or reshuffle! or resign! or form or formation and date aft [two weeks before the appointment] and date bef [two weeks after the appointment].

Inevitably, the search results included articles unrelated to the event analyzed. All search results were carefully scrutinized in determining the final count.

The analysis included articles that discussed coalition announcements, the presentation of the cabinet to parliament, announcement of appointments, profiles of cabinet ministers, demands for resignations, leadership struggles or challenges within the parties in government, or speculation about appointments (such as "Chirac Likely Choice for Next Prime Minister").

Excluded from consideration were articles that discussed the presentation of the government's program or budget to parliament, opposition parties' leadership selections, the opening of parliament, currency reactions to changes in government, and general international opinion of government choices (such as the U.S. response to the inclusion of the French Communist Party in a leftist coalition: "President Bush Says Appointment of Communists Bound to Cause Concern among Allies").

Notes

Chapter 1. Introduction

1. *Parliamentary system* refers to the unique institutional and behavioral patterns in which there is no effective separation between the legislative and executive branches of government. These systems give pride of place to political parties and parliamentary elections (Gallagher et al. 1992). *Parliamentary-type system* refers to France, which has a unique variant of the parliamentary system that some have termed a hybrid system. The French system blends parliamentarianism with an American-style presidency (Gallagher et al. 1992).

2. See, however, Martin (1989) and Carroll (1984) for two notable exceptions.

3. In addition to these two schools of cabinet studies, there are efforts to bridge the gap between them (for two excellent examples, see Laver and Schofield 1990 and Budge and Keman 1990).

4. Portfolios are the job responsibilities of ministers. They usually correspond to, though are not limited to, government departments, headed by a cabinet member. Some members of the cabinet, designated ministers without portfolio, either have no specific administrative area or are charged with responsibility for a matter that is not supervised by a formal government department.

5. He describes how Wilson and Heath merged many government departments into "super-departments" and developed a second tier of ministers under the secretaries of state (Rose 1987). Previously, the British cabinet had had a "two-class" structure: senior ministers, designated as secretaries of state, and "ministers not in the cabinet," responsible for government departments that were not part of the cabinet structure. The creation of superministries under Heath and Wilson and the emergence of a two-tier system are not fundamentally different from the former two-class system. In the new system, the ministers of state (junior ministers) have status comparable to that of the former second class of ministers. However, the new junior ministers do not have formal responsibility for a department as did their predecessors. Instead, their respon-

sibility within the department is not clearly defined. (See Rose [1987] for a complete discussion of the history of the British cabinet structure.)

6. Good discussions of the first wave of feminism in Western Europe are found in Lovenduski (1986) and Randall (1987).

7. Recent scholarship also argues that the term *second wave* inaccurately suggests a disjuncture between early feminist activities and accomplishments and the later ones (see, for example, Randall 1987).

8. In some cantons, it appears, women still do not have the right to vote (Kaplan 1992, 140).

9. The protections and policies of the Swedish state, coveted by many women around the world, are the result of the efforts of Swedish women (Gelb 1989; Kaplan 1992). Similarly, the second wave in France and the Netherlands has been marked by accomplishments for women out of all proportion to the strength of their movements (Lovenduski 1986; Kaplan 1992).

10. Although abortion at first mobilized and unified women, it eventually contributed to deep divisions among them by raising fundamental issues surrounding the nature of womanhood and the place of motherhood (Randall 1987).

11. Wilcox uses Euro-barometer data for 1975, 1983, and 1987. His cases include Belgium, Denmark, France, West Germany, Italy, Ireland, Netherlands, United Kingdom. Interestingly, Wilcox (1991) finds that public opinion on family roles has remained more persistently inegalitarian than the attitude toward women in the political arena. For example, Irish respondents in his study were more supportive of women in the public realm than in the private one. Contrary to the general trend, the Italian public tended to have more egalitarian attitudes toward women in private life than in the political realm. Wilcox also finds that in West Germany, Italy, Ireland, and Belgium, women were more supportive than men of women in public life. In Denmark, such gender gaps in support for women in office were absent.

12. The traditional gender gap in Western Europe—which has led to women being more inclined to support conservative rather than leftist parties—may be changing. In recent years, several scholars have noted that Western European women tend to embrace more leftist positions than do men on a number of issues (Norris 1985a, 1988; Welch and Thomas 1988; Wilcox 1991). Because some have noted that women continue to locate ideologically to the right of men yet have tended to hold more liberal positions, one study argues that the very meaning of left and right may be different for men than for women (Jelen, Thomas, and Wilcox 1994).

13. Briefly, the New Politics argument is that recent generations of Western publics, who have greater resources than past generations, are more likely to engage in elite-directing than in elite-directed activities (see Inglehart 1990; Dalton 1988; Dalton et al. 1984).

14. Note that even in those systems where a parliamentary seat and a cabinet portfolio are incompatible, parliamentary membership usually precedes cabinet appoint-

ment. In such systems, it is usually upon appointment that ministers resign their parliamentary mandates.

15. *Critical mass*, a term borrowed from physics, denotes that quantity of a catalyst needed to induce a nonreversible chain reaction (Dahlerup 1988).

16. In political tactics, women's organizations that seek to augment the number of women in government frequently mimic minority groups. For example, the bargaining of the women's caucuses of the political parties of several Scandinavian countries to pressure the parties to accept goals (quotas) for inclusion of women resembles the 1988 maneuvering of American minorities to assure greater representation in the Democratic National Committee in the United States. An understanding of the causes of change in the inclusion of women in government, therefore, may shed light on mechanisms that may bring about a greater representation of other groups who also hold only a minority of power.

Chapter 2. Participation of Women in Government

1. In most countries, the person charged with responsibility for a specific government department is called a minister, and a second tier of persons with lesser responsibility are called secretaries of state. In the United Kingdom, though, this nomenclature is the reverse: secretaries of state head ministries, assisted by ministers. In some countries, the cabinet is called the Council of Ministers (as in Austria, France, Germany). In France, the term *cabinet* refers to the personal staffs attached to ministers (Thiebault 1988). I use the term *cabinet* to mean the highest executive or the Council of Ministers, rather than the ministerial staffs.

2. The Irish cabinet system was born of different historical circumstances. It predates the establishment of the Republic of Ireland. De Valera and the Sinn Féin party created an Irish state having British structures following the founding of the Dail in 1918. The almost wholesale adoption of British institutions may account for the Irish cabinet system being "More British than the British Themselves" (Farrell 1988, 33).

3. In this respect, cabinets are like parties, being central to democracy yet receiving scant constitutional notice. In this respect, cabinets are very similar to the modern White House staff.

4. One outgrowth has been the development in most political arenas of a more specialized cabinet committee system (James 1992; Blondel 1988). The cabinet committee system has undertaken much of the decision making and policy making that in prior eras took place collectively. Cabinet committees also play an essential coordinating role among ministries (Blondel 1988). Despite the devolution of cabinet work to committees, cabinets have remained the paramount institution in parliamentary democracies (James 1992).

5. What has been most debated in the British case is whether power within cabinets has been consolidated into the hands of prime ministers. In many countries of a more corporatist nature, it has been suggested that parliaments have declined not vis-à-vis

the executive but vis-à-vis the extragovernmental corporatist bodies. Because the participation of women in government has been highest in some of the countries in which corporatist structures are strongest, some have cynically suggested that women have been able to move into the legislative and executive branches of government because power is no longer situated in these institutions.

6. Harold Wilson (1976) writes that during his seven years, eight months in the premiership, he answered more than twelve thousand parliamentary questions.

7. Dogan (1989) treats the appointment of ministers by prime ministers in his excellent discussion of the various recruitment norms of cabinet accession in several countries. He suggests that the official nomination by the prime minister in most cases is a fiction masking the true selection process, in which many people and many constraints play a role.

8. Rose (1987) operationalizes the hierarchies of the British cabinet system using four criteria: the amount of parliamentary attention a ministry receives; the amount of media attention devoted to the ministry; the extent to which the ministry has been used in the past as a steppingstone to higher office; and the authority within the cabinet. Aside from the problematic nature of the third criterion, this represents one of the more systematic attempts to distinguish among ministries.

9. For an interesting exception, see the cabinet of Prime Minister Ingvar Carlsson of Sweden (*Keesing's Contemporary Archives*, Jan. 1990, 37197). Carlsson explicitly designates an inner cabinet, comprising the Ministries of Finance, Justice, Labor, Industry, and Foreign Affairs. Members of the inner cabinet were to coordinate the work of the cabinet's three working groups.

10. Note that the nomenclature can be somewhat confusing. See chap.2, n.1.

11. The composition of cabinets varies both cross-nationally and temporally. In some cases, both junior- and senior-level ministers are designated cabinet members. In others, senior ministers only are considered cabinet members. Some countries have added junior ministers to their cabinets in recent years as part of an effort to manage increased levels of government responsibility (Blondel and Müller-Rommel 1988). The cabinet composition—whether it includes or excludes junior ministers—reflects that reported by *Keesing's Contemporary Archives*.

12. Because cabinet members often are charged with the leadership of more than one department, the number of portfolios in a cabinet usually exceeds the number of ministries. Each functional designation attached to a minister was coded as a separate portfolio.

13. This study, focused on Western Europe, does not address cabinet appointments in the United States. Consistent with the pattern reported by Martin (1989), women in the United States are most likely to receive appointments in the outer circle of departments.

14. A related argument suggests that organizational norms may persist or be reasserted through informal mechanisms long after formal obstacles to inclusion have

been removed (Considine and Deutchman 1993; Blalock 1967; Reskin 1988). For this reason, minority-group members are unable to transform institutions when their presence is small in number or short in historical duration (Considine and Deutchman 1993; Thomas 1994; Kanter 1975; but see also Yoder 1991).

15. As discussed more fully in chap. 3, Kanter's (1977) work has led many to believe that 35 percent is the magic turning point for minority groups such that when their numerical presence exceeds 35 percent, they are able to effect significant change on the institutional culture. Recently the idea of investing any specific percentage with that meaning has been questioned (Considine and Deutchman 1993; Blalock 1967; Reskin 1988; Thomas 1994; Yoder 1991; Dahlerup 1988).

16. Nowhere during the time frame of this study were any of the deputy prime ministers female. In some systems, deputy prime ministers are generalists whose main role is that of party watchdog (Blondel 1988). In other systems, deputy prime ministers are leaders of coalition parties not holding the premiership. This is the case, for example, in Belgium (Frognier 1988). The infrequency of women as party leaders, then, is part of the reason why they have had no appointments as deputy prime ministers.

17. In the United States, for example, Governor Anne Richards of Texas has been one such female executive (Witt, Paget, and Matthews 1994).

18. The sex of a prime minister has been coded 1 for men and 2 for women, so that a positive correlation between the sex of a prime minister and women in government signifies an association of female prime ministers with greater numbers of women in government.

19. Many feminists have argued that the frequent question of whether women in office make a difference is offensive in itself since we rarely ask men to justify their political presence. This said, it should be noted that the question is indeed an interesting empirical one that is being addressed by a number of scholars (notably Thomas 1994; Reingold 1991). It is a question to which the analysis will return in chapter 4.

20. Note that this suggests that the concept of leadership is gender neutral, a notion that many would challenge (see, for example, Cantor and Bernay 1992).

21. Witt et al. (1994) point out that the mother of a young child remains a curiosity in political office in the 1990s. They highlight the media attention directed at Carol Browner, appointed by President Clinton in 1993 to direct the Environmental Protection Agency, who was confirmed with a baby in her arms.

22. A district candidacy meeting is a meeting of those party members in a political district in the United Kingdom who are responsible for "adopting" (choosing) a candidate to be the party's standard-bearer in that district in upcoming general elections.

23. *Fraktionen* are party working groups or caucuses. They are the organizing unit of the Bundestag.

24. Although party discipline is significantly weaker in the United States, thereby creating the potential for female legislators to have more dissimilar voting behavior than their male counterparts, Smeal's cautionary interpretation of voting records is still well taken for the Europeanist.

25. It is perhaps because of this last dilemma that the 1979 election campaign of Thatcher (the "Iron Lady") was colored by strong references to her traditional female roles as wife and mother (Gelb 1989).

26. One issue that remains unclear in the literature is how women's greater numeric presence within legislatures translates into a heightened policy impact. Greater numbers of women in office may alter intrainstitutional dynamics. There is also the possibility, though, that greater policy attention for issues affecting women's lives may result from the societal changes that first lead to women's greater numeric representation. Thomas (1994) argues that women in the United States have been freer to represent women substantively as American society has become less ambivalent about the role of women in public life.

27. Notably, many question the wisdom of basing arguments for representation on the matter of difference. Historically, "difference" has been evoked to justify discrimination and exclusion (Witt, Paget, and Matthews 1994).

28. Brundtland's priorities for government have included provision of child care and kindergartens, the environment, maternity leave, and nature preserves—in addition to traditional labor policies of full employment. The number of women appointed to her government in 1986—seven, or 43 percent of all ministers—was a world record (Davis 1995).

Chapter 3. The Pool of Eligibles

1. One small part of Salazar's legacy has been high illiteracy rates, no doubt at least in part a result of the inadequacy of educational infrastructure. Portuguese illiteracy rates have been rapidly falling as the new regime has operated schools in shifts, in some places keeping them open until 11:00 P.M. Still, the 1988 illiteracy rate for women (21 percent) was considerably higher than for men (11 percent) (Kaplan 1992).

2. According to Kaplan (1992, 182), the law exiled a man from his province for three months for committing such a murder. The punishment for terminating a pregnancy, in contrast, was eight years.

3. For a contrasting argument, see Togeby (1994). Her work argues that dramatic changes in workforce participation have led to a radicalization of the female electorate in Denmark. Although her study suggests that changed workforce participation is responsible for gender gaps in political values, alternative explanations for observed differences between men and women are not adequately explored.

4. Helga Nowotny's (1981) study supports this argument. She claims that women have been able to accumulate only certain types of political capital, that the rules for conversion of political capital are different for men and for women, and that women frequently cannot access the appropriate networking channels in which to convert their capital.

5. In fact, some political systems require that a person, once appointed to the cabinet, must resign from his or her seat in the parliament. (This is the case in France, Nor-

way, Sweden, and the Netherlands.) Moreover, in Ireland, where the constitution requires cabinet ministers to be members of the Dail, parliament nonetheless has the authority to bypass this requirement and to appoint nonparliamentary experts.

6. The term *backbencher* is country-specific, referring to members of the British House of Commons who literally sit on the bench at the rear of the chamber. The term designates those junior parliament members who do not hold government positions.

Chapter 4. Recruitment Norms

1. Note that de Winter (1991) uses different terminology for the same distinction. What are here termed generalist systems he calls parliamentary; specialist systems he terms semiparliamentary. I follow Blondel in embracing the generalist/specialist terminology.

2. Wilson also notes that in the interests of appointing a cabinet representative of the party as well as responsive to parliament and the nation, a prime minister needs a keen "forgettory" of past grudges and quarrels (1976, 30).

3. Lijphart (1968, 1977, 1984) defines *consociationalism* as a system of democratic maintenance in highly plural cultures—fragmented cultures, in Eckstein's (1975) sense—in which elite representatives of the cultural groups communicate, cooperate, and bargain in an effort to ensure the mutual interests of the various groups. Consociational democracies are characterized by grand coalitions, mutual vetoes, proportional-representation electoral systems, and party pacts (which are explicit though not always publicly explicated or justified).

4. A private member's bill is sponsored by an individual member of parliament rather than by the British government. It is not referred to as a private member bill in all parliamentary democracies. However, just as in the United Kingdom, in most parliamentary democracies it is unusual for legislation sponsored by individuals rather than by parties or governments to be successful.

5. Searing uses this wonderfully apt metaphor, referring to gender, without ever discussing gender or the gendered implications of what he says.

6. Separate inclusion of each of the three recruitment indicators in a regression model would no doubt produce significant problems with multicollinearity because the three indicators are highly intercorrelated. Exclusion of any one of them, on the other hand, leaves specification problems.

Party leadership, following de Winter (1991), means any position in the national, regional, or local executive organs of a political party.

Data on the three characteristics are from de Winter's (1991) average for the postwar period for each of the countries. Because de Winter's analysis extends back to 1945, the newer Western European democracies—Spain, Portugal, and Greece—were not included in his study. Lacking a comparable measure for these cases, I omitted them from this analysis. Even if I did have access to comparable data, however, there are reasons to question whether the typology I have here developed would be useful for these three cases. Average parliamentary tenure rates, for example, are likely to be considerably depressed, especially for cases in the late 1970s and early 1980s, because of the limited experience of these countries with parliamentary democracy.

7. Weighted least squares regression, rather than ordinary least squares, was used because of the observation of slight heteroskedastic error patterns. Data were weighted by the error.

8. Although political culture is a very broad concept, I am here interested in only one specific aspect of it. I will therefore adopt Norris's (1993) definition of political culture: "the dominant values and attitudes towards the role of women in society and in political life."

9. Euro-barometer data do not provide a satisfactory measure of political culture because not every survey asks the same questions. Further, some of the fifteen countries in this study are not included in Euro-barometer surveys because they are outside the European Union at the time of this writing.

10. This dummy variable is coded 1 if the region is Scandinavia and 0 if not.

11. Preferential voting arrangements allow voters to strike some candidates' names from a proportional representation list in favor of other candidates. In a variation called bullet voting, all of a person's votes go for a single candidate on the list. In a widely publicized door-to-door campaign, female activists in Norway in the 1970s recruited other women to use preferential voting by striking men's names from the ballot in favor of women's names (Bystydienski 1988). Because of what happened in Norway, preferential voting arrangements are frequently cited as electoral configurations favorable to women, but as this discussion demonstrates, they can as likely be used against women as for them.

12. Specifically, Matland's work finds that the district magnitude and party magnitude are key.

13. Some may question whether it is appropriate to group Denmark with Scandinavia or with continental Europe for the purposes of this analysis. Although Wilcox (1991) does not discuss Scandinavian countries because of his reliance on Euro-barometer data, his findings repeatedly demonstrate that Denmark has a significantly higher level of support than other European countries for equality of opportunity for women. The findings support my decision to include Denmark in the Nordic rather than the continental region.

Chapter 5. The Party-Parliament Nexus

1. The parliamentary party is the subgroup of a political party that has been elected to the parliament. Or, when conceptualized as a subgroup of parliament, the parliamentary party is all MPs who belong to the same party.

2. See for example MacDonald's (1989) separate analyses of the British Labour and Conservative parties.

3. Ironically, women's votes, historically conservative, had prevented Mitterand from coming to power in prior elections (Kaplan 1992).

4. *Safe seats* in parliament are those that are won in electoral contests, being located in districts in which the party has a stronghold. In the case of these seats, selection equals election since there is no risk that the party will fail in that district. *Marginal seats* are those that are potentially winnable but likely to be won only after a difficult electoral contest. *Hopeless seats* are those that the party has, based on traditional levels of support among that particular constituency, almost no chance of winning.

5. Richard Rose (1971) notes the tendency in England for the Labour Party to make greater efforts to be representative in cabinet formation than does the Conservative Party. He points out that Labour cabinets tend to include "a Cooperator, a woman, and a prominent trade unionist, as well as a Scot and a Welshman" (397). However, his description of Labour's geographical, occupational, and gender inclusion might seem to some to resemble tokenism more than true interest balancing.

6. See Wilma Rule's (1981, 1989) discussion of the case of the United States. She finds that at the state level, being a Democrat was disadvantageous to female political candidates during the 1970s but not during the 1980s.

7. Norris and Lovenduski (1992) use the language of supply and demand to discuss whether the different rates at which parties within Great Britain slate women for electoral competition are the result of a lack of women who want to run or the result of party selectorate discrimination. They find that it is primarily supply factors—the absence of women presenting themselves as candidates—that result in so few being adopted as candidates. They do, however, note that supply and demand are not unrelated. Women may be reluctant to step forward to run because of the perception that their applications for candidacy will not be treated fairly.

8. I gratefully acknowledge the assistance of Christina Pintat of the Inter-Parliamentary Union for providing data and assistance in gathering data.

9. Correlation between a party's left/right placement and the indicator of left/right placement of the coalition is strong and significant ($p = .6041$). Including both in the model allows an examination of the possibility that party behavior may be conditioned by coalitional norms.

10. Rather than the number of women in government, the percentage of women in government could have been used as the dependent variable. This alternative, however, would have introduced significant methodological problems, not the least of which would result from the narrow range of variation among governments in this study.

11. It has previously been shown that in terms of women's appointment to office, there are significant differences between the period of a new government and that of a reshuffle (see Davis and Lancaster 1993).

12. Earlier, ordinary least squares analyses revealed problems with heteroskedastic patterns in the error. Analyses reported here have accordingly been weighted by the error term.

13. A surplus majority coalition is one that includes more parties than are necessary to obtain the support of a working majority of parliamentary deputies.

14. Karen Beckwith (1989) notes the absence of anything a priori advantageous to women in the nature of institutional arrangements such as proportional representation. She argues that, lacking a commitment to the recruitment of women, political parties will not use specific types of institutional arrangements to promote women to office.

Chapter 6. The Electoral Cycle of Appointments

1. Wilcox (1991) does not find similar levels of support in the European publics for private role equality. There is a considerable degree of belief among the publics he studied that women should have less demanding jobs and should be responsible for a greater proportion of the domestic labor than men.

2. News articles were counted for only those cabinet reorganizations after 1980 because Reuters and UPI were not on-line until the fall of 1980 (Reuters went on-line 15 April 1979 and UPI went on-line 26 September 1980). Although both these news services publish indexes for the earlier periods, only computer searches were done because I could not be certain of generating comparable counts of news articles for the period before on-line operations. For the analyses that follow, country-specific averages were generated using SAS and substituted for the pre-1980 period, thereby making possible the inclusion of pre-1980 cases. For comparison purposes, all analyses were run each way (either excluding the pre-1980 cases and or including the pre-1980 averages). Retaining the pre-1980 cases using the country-specific averages in no way did violence to the analyses. The performance of the variables or the models was unaltered.

3. Wilcox (1994) argues that redistricting—which also affected incumbency—and the record number of women willing to run for office were also key factors in the electoral success of women in 1992. Redistricting resulted, for example, in many "incumbents" running in districts in which they had never before campaigned.

4. One problem associated with logistic regression is that there is no measure of association for the model as a whole that performs satisfactorily. We have no satisfactory measure corresponding to the R^2 of regression. Nonetheless, two measures of association are reported: gama (.649) and a pseudo R^2, R_L^2, (.285). Gamma is notoriously inflated; the R_L^2 has been shown consistently to underestimate the performance of the model. The performance of the model as a whole explains between 29 and 65 percent of the variance associated with the dependent variable, the likelihood of a woman being appointed. Even by conservative measures, then, the model is robust.

5. The parameter estimate is converted to the percentage change in the log odds of a woman being appointed by using the following formula (Demaris 1992), where b_j is the parameter estimate: Percent change in log odds = $100 [\exp (b_j) -1]$.

Chapter 7. Conclusion

1. When female ministers receive media attention, however, the content of that attention is often significantly different from that focused on male politicians (Witt and

Paget 1984; Kanter 1977; Davis 1995). That is, media focus on female politicians often reflects scrutiny of their personal lives in a way that is not characteristic of the coverage of male politicians. This difference suggests a need for further study of the media attention devoted to female politicians.

2. Discussing recruitment patterns as being either generalist or specialist is a dichotomization in an attempt to simplify ideal types for analytical purposes. In fact, however, there are a range of recruitment patterns.

References

Aberbach, Joel D., Robert D. Putnam, and Bert A. Rockman. 1981. *Bureaucrats and Politicians in Western Democracies*. Cambridge: Harvard University Press.

Alderman, R. K., and J. A. Cross. 1981. "Patterns of Ministerial Turnover in Two Labour Cabinets." *Political Studies*, 34 (3): 425–30.

———. 1985. "The Reluctant Knife: Reflections on the PM's Power of Dismissal." *Parliamentary Affairs* 38 (4): 387–408.

———. 1986. "Rejuvenating the Cabinet: The Record of Post-war British Prime Ministers Compared." *Political Studies* 34: 639–46.

———. 1987. "The Timing of Cabinet Reshuffles." *Parliamentary Affairs* 40 (1): 1–19.

Allison, Paul D. 1990. *Event History Analysis: Regression for Longitudinal Event Data*. Newbury Park CA: Sage.

Almond, Gabriel A., and Sidney Verba. 1963. *The Civic Culture: Political Attitudes and Democracy in Five Nations*. Princeton: Princeton University Press.

Anderson, Kristi. 1975. "Working Women and Political Participation: 1952–1972." *American Journal of Political Science* 19 (August): 439–53.

Anderson, Kristi, and Stuart Thorson. 1984. "Some Structural Barriers to the Election of Women to Congress: A Simulation." *Western Political Quarterly* 37: 143–56.

Andeweg, R. B. 1988a. "Centrifugal Forces and Collective Decision-Making: The Case of the Dutch Cabinet." *European Journal of Political Research* 16 (2): 125–51.

———. 1988b. "The Netherlands." In Blondel and Müller-Rommel 1988, 47–67.

Appleton, Andrew, and Amy G. Mazur. 1993. "Transformation or Modernization: Rhetoric and Reality of Gender and Party Politics in France." In Lovenduski and Norris 1993, 86–112.

Arter, David. 1985. "Government in Finland: A 'Semi-Presidential System'?" *Parliamentary Affairs* 38 (4): 472–95.

Astelarra, Judith. 1992. "Women, Political Culture, and Empowerment in Spain." In Bystydzienski 1992, 41–50.

Bagehot, W. 1963. *The English Constitution*. London: Fontana.

Bar, Antonio. 1988. "Spain." In Blondel and Müller-Rommel 1988, 102–19.

Beckwith, Karen. 1980. "The Cross-Cultural Study of Women and Politics: Methodological Problems." *Women and Politics* 1 (2): 7–28.

——. 1985. "Feminism and Leftist Politics in Italy: The Case of UDI-PCI Relations." *West European Politics* 8 (4): 19–37.

——. 1989. "Sneaking Women into Office: Alternative Access to Parliament in France and Italy." *Women and Politics* 9 (3): 1–15.

Bernstein, Robert. 1986. "Why Are There So Few Women in the House?" *Western Political Quarterly* 39: 155–63.

Biersack, Robert, and Paul S. Herrnson. 1994. "Political Parties and the Year of the Woman." In *The Year of the Woman: Myths and Realities*, ed. Elizabeth Adell Cook, Sue Thomas, and Clyde Wilcox. Boulder CO: Westview.

Birch, A. H. 1989. "Responsibility in British Politics." In *Ministerial Responsibility*, ed. Geoffrey Marshall. New York: Oxford University Press.

Blalock, Hubert. 1967. *Toward a Theory of Minority-Group Relations*. New York: Wiley.

Blondel, Jean. 1985. *Government Ministers in the Contemporary World*. London: Sage.

——. 1988. "Introduction: Western European Cabinets in Comparative Perspective." In Blondel and Müller-Rommel 1988, 1–16.

——. 1991. "Introduction." In Blondel and Thiebault 1991, 1–4.

Blondel, Jean, and Ferdinand Müller-Rommel, eds. 1988. *Cabinets in Western Europe*. London: MacMillan.

Bloden, Jean, and Jean-Louis Thiebault, eds. 1991. *The Profession of Government Minister in Western Europe*. London: MacMillan.

Bochel, J. M., and D. T. Denver. 1983. "Candidate Selection in the Labour Party: What the Selectors Seek," *British Journal of Politics* 13: 45–69.

Brodie, M. Janine. 1985. *Women and Politics in Canada*. Toronto: McGraw-Hill Ryerson.

Brown, Michele, and Ann O'Connor. 1986. *Hammer and Tongues: The Best of Women's Wit and Humor*. New York: McGraw-Hill.

Budge, Ian, and Hans J. Keman. 1990. *Parties and Democracy: Coalition Formation and Government Functioning in Twenty States*. New York: Oxford University Press.

Bumiller, Elisabeth. 1990. *May You Be the Mother of a Hundred Sons: A Journey among the Women of India*. New York: Fawcett Columbine.

Burch, Philip H., Jr. 1980. *Elites in American History: The New Deal to the Carter Administration*. New York: Holmes and Meier.

Burrell, Barbara. 1994. *A Woman's Place Is in the House: Campaigning for Congress in the Feminist Era*. Ann Arbor: University of Michigan Press.

Bystydzienski, Jill M. 1988. "Women in Politics in Norway," *Women in Politics* 8 (3/4): 73–95.

———. 1992a. "Influence of Women's Culture on Public Politics in Norway." In Bystydzienski 1992b, 11–23.

Bystydzienski, Jill M., ed. 1992b. *Women Transforming Politics*. Bloomington: Indiana University Press.

Calvert, Peter, ed. 1987. *The Process of Political Succession*. London: MacMillan.

Cameron, David R. 1982. "On the Limits of the Public Economy." *The Annals of the American Academy of Political and Social Science* 459: 46–62.

———. 1984. "Social Democracy, Corporatism, and Labor Quiescence: The Representation of Economic Interest in Advanced Capitalist Society." In *Order and Conflict in Contemporary Capitalism*, ed. John H. Goldthorpe. New York: Oxford University Press.

Cantor, Dorothy W., and Toni Bernay. 1992. *Women in Power: The Secrets of Leadership*. New York: Houghton Mifflin.

Carroll, Susan. 1984. "The Recruitment of Women for Cabinet-Level Posts in State Government: A Social Control Perspective." *Social Science Journal* 21 (1): 91–107.

———. 1989. "The Personal Is Political: The Intersection of Private Lives and Public Roles among Women and Men in Elective and Appointive Office." *Women and Politics* 9 (2): 51–67.

———. 1990. "Looking Back at the 1980s and Forward to the 1990s." CAWP *News and Notes* 7 (summer): 9–12.

———. 1994. *Women as Candidates in the U.S.* 2nd ed. Bloomington: Indiana University Press.

Carty, R. Kenneth, and Lynda Erickson. 1991. "Candidate Nomination in Canada's National Political Parties." In *Canadian Political Parties: Leaders, Candidates and Organizaton*, ed. Herman Bakvis. Vol. 13. Toronto: Dundurn.

Castles, Barbara. 1980. *The Castle Diaries 1974–76*. London: Weidenfeld and Nicolson.

Castles, Francis G., and Peter Mair. 1984. "Left-Right Political Scales: Some 'Expert' Judgments." *European Journal of Political Research* 12: 73–88.

Christy, Carol A. 1984. "Economic Development and Sex Differences in Political Participation." *Women and Politics* 4 (1): 7–34.

———. 1985. "American and German Trends in Sex Differences in Political Participation." *Comparative Political Studies* 18: 81–103.

Coakley, John. 1984. "Selecting a PM: The Irish Experience." *Parliamentary Affairs* 37 (4): 403–17.

Coleman, Fred. 1994. "Political Power Is Only Half the Battle: Norwegian Women Still Lag in the Workplace." *U.S. News and World Report*, 13 June, 58.

Considine, Mark, and Iva Ellen Deutchman. 1993. "Instituting Gender: State Legislators in Australia and the United States." Paper presented at the 1993 annual meeting of the American Political Science Association, Washington DC.

Cotta, Maurizio. 1991. "Conclusion." In Blondel and Theibault 1991, 174–98.

Cox, D. R., and E. J. Snell. 1989. *Analysis of Binary Data.* 2nd ed. London: Chapman and Hall.

Dahlerup, Drude. 1988. "From a Small to a Large Minority: Women in Scandinavian Politics." *Scandinavian Political Studies* 11 (4): 275–97.

Dahlerup, Drude, and Brita Gulli. 1985. "Women's Organizations in the Nordic Countries: Lack of Force or Counterforce?" In Haavio-Mannila et al. 1985, 6–36.

Dahlerup, Drude, and Elina Haavio-Mannila. 1985. "Summary." In Haavio-Mannila et al. 1985, 160–69.

Dalton, Russell. 1988. *Citizen Politics in Western Democracies.* Chatham NJ: Chatham House.

———. 1989. *Politics in West Germany.* Boston: Scott Foresman.

Dalton, Russell, S. C. Flanagan, and P. A. Beck. 1984. *Electoral Change in Advanced Industrial Democracies.* Princeton: Princeton University Press.

Darcy, R., Susan Welch, and Janet Clark. 1994. *Women, Elections, and Representation.* 2nd ed. New York: Longman.

Davis, Rebecca Howard. 1995. "Gro Harlem Brundtland." In *Political Leaders of Contemporary Western Europe,* ed. David Wilsford. Westport CT: Greenwood Press.

Davis, Rebecca Howard, and Thomas D. Lancaster. 1993. "The Electoral Cycle of Appointments: Timing, Incumbency, and the Appointment of Women." Paper presented at the annual meeting of the American Political Science Association, Washington DC.

Day, Alan, ed. 1988. *Political Parties of the World.* 3rd ed. Essex UK: Longman.

De Beauvoir, Simone. 1984. "France: Feminism—Alive, Well, and in Constant Danger." In *Sisterhood Is Global,* ed. R. Morgan. New York: Anchor.

Demaris, Alfred. 1992. *Logit Modeling: Practical Applications.* Newbury Park CA: Sage.

de Winter, Lieven. 1991. "Parliamentary and Party Pathways to the Cabinet." In Blondel and Theibault 1991, 44–69.

Diamond, Irene. 1977. *Sex Roles in the State House.* New Haven: Yale University Press.

Dicey, A. V. 1989. "Ministerial Responsibility and the Rule of Law." In *Ministerial Responsibility,* ed. Geoffrey Marshall. New York: Oxford University Press.

Dodd, Lawrence. 1984. "The Study of Cabinet Durability: Introduction and Commentary." *Comparative Political Studies* 17 (2): 155–61.

Dodson, Debra. 1989. "A Comparison of the Impact of Women and Men's Attitudes on Their Legislative Behavior: Is What They Say What They Do?" Paper presented at the annual meeting of the American Political Science Association, Atlanta GA.

Dogan, Mattei, ed. 1975. *The Mandarins of Western Europe: The Political Role of Top Civil Servants*. New York: John Wiley.

———. 1989. "Introduction: Selecting Cabinet Ministers" and "How to Become a Cabinet Minister in Italy." In *Pathways to Power: Selecting Rulers in Pluralist Democracies*, 1–18 and 99–139. Boulder CO: Westview.

Duverger, Maurice. 1955. *The Political Role of Women*. Paris: UNESCO.

Dye, T. 1976. *Policy Analysis*. Alabama: University of Alabama Press.

Eduards, Maud, Beatrice Halsaa, and Hege Skjeie. 1985. "Equality: How Equal." In Elina Haavio-Mannila et al. 1985, 134–59.

Ehrmann, Henry W. 1983. *Politics in France*. Boston: Little Brown.

Einhorn, Barbara. 1993. *Cinderella Goes to Market: Citizenship, Gender, and Women's Movements in East Central Europe*. New York: Verso.

Ellis, David. 1989. "Collective Ministerial Responsibility and Collective Solidarity." In *Ministerial Responsibility*, ed. Geoffrey Marshall. New York: Oxford University Press.

Enloe, Cynthia. 1989. *Bananas, Beaches, and Bases: Making Feminist Sense of International Relations*. Berkeley: University of California Press.

Evans, Richard. 1987. *Comrades and Sisters: Feminism, Socialism and Pacificism in Europe, 1870–1945*. New York: St. Martin's.

Farrell, Brian. 1988. "Ireland. The Irish Cabinet System: More British than the British Themselves." In Blondel and Müller-Rommel 1988, 33–46.

Frognier, André Paul. 1988. "Belgium: A Complex Cabinet in a Fragmented Polity." In Blondel and Müller-Rommel 1988, 68–85.

———. 1991. "Elite Circulation in Cabinet Government." In Blondel and Thiebault 1991, 119–35.

Gallagher, Michael, Michael Laver, and Peter Mair. 1992. *Representative Government in Western Europe*. New York: McGraw Hill.

Galligan, Yvonne. 1993. "Party Politics and Gender in the Republic of Ireland." In Lovenduski and Norris 1993, 147–67.

Gelb, Joyce. 1989. *Feminism and Politics: A Comparative Perspective*. Berkeley: University of California Press.

Gerlich, Peter, and Wolfgang C. Müller. 1988. "Austria: Routine and Ritual." In Blondel and Müller-Rommel 1988, 138–50.

Gerzog, Irwin N. 1984. *Congressional Women: Their Recruitment, Treatment and Behavior*. New York: Praeger.

Graves, Pamela. 1994. *Labour Women: Women in British Working-Class Politics, 1918–1939*. New York: Cambridge University Press.

Grofman, Bernard, and Arend Lijphart, eds. 1986. *Electoral Laws and Their Political Consequences*. New York: Agathon.

Guadagnini, Marila. 1993. "A 'Partitocrazia' without Women: The Case of the Italian Party System." In Lovenduski and Norris 1993, 168–204.

Gudmundsdóttir, Esther, Gun Hedlunk-Ruth, Janneke van der Ros Schive, Torild Skard, and Ulla Wamberg. 1985. "Women in Local Politics." In Haavio-Mannila et al. 1985, 81–105.

Haavio-Mannila, Elina, Drude Dahlerup, Maud Eduards, Esther Gudmundsdottir, Beatrice Halsaa, Helga Maria Hernes, Evan Hanninen-Salmelin, Bergthora Sigmundsdottir, Sirkka Sinkkonen, and Torild Skard, eds. 1985. *Unfinished Democracy: Women in Nordic Politics*. New York: Pergamon.

Haavio-Mannila, Elina, and Torild Skard. 1985. "The Arena for Political Activity: The Position of Women in the Nordic Societies Today." In Haavio-Mannila, et al. 1985, 1–5.

Halsaa, Beatrice, Helga Maria Hernes, and Sirkka Sinkkonen. 1985. "Introduction." In Haavio-Mannila, et al. 1985, xv–xix.

Hansen, Preben, Bent Tying, and Thorkild Borre, eds. 1985. *Women in Denmark in the 1980s*. Copenhagen: Royal Danish Ministry of Foreign Affairs.

Hernes, Helga Marie. 1984. "Women in the Corporate Channel." In *The Situation of Women in Political Process in Europe*. Preliminary report submitted to the Council of Europe. Strasbourg: Directorate of Human Rights, Council of Europe.

Hernes, Helga Marie, and Eva Hänninen-Salmelin. 1985. "Women in the Corporate System." In Haavio-Mannila et al. 1985, 106–33.

Hills, J. 1981. "Candidates: The Impact of Gender." *Parliamentary Affairs* 34: 221–28.

———. 1983. "Life-Style Constraints on Formal Political Participation—Why So Few Women Local Councillors in Britain?" *Electoral Studies* 2 (1): 39–52.

Inglehart, Margaret L. 1981. "Political Interest in West European Women: An Historical and Empirical Comparative Analysis." *Comparative Political Studies* 14; 299–326.

Inglehart, Ronald. 1977. *The Silent Revolution*. Princeton: Princeton University Press.

———. 1990. *Culture Shift*. Princeton: Princeton University Press.

International Labour Organization. 1990. "Total and Economically Active Population by Sex and Age Group." In *Yearbook of Labour Statistics: Retrospective Edition on Population Census: 1945–1989*, 78–110. Geneva: ILO.

Inter-Parliamentary Union (IPU). 1991. *Distribution of Seats betweeen Men and Women in National Parliaments: Statistical Data from 1945 to 30 June 1991*. Geneva: IPU.

———. 1992. *Women and Political Power: Survey Carried Out among the 150 National Parliaments Existing as of 31 October 1991*. Reports and Documents series no. 19. Geneva: IPU.

Jackman, Robert. 1980. "Socialist Parties and Income Inequalities in Western Industrial Societies." *Journal of Politics* 42 (1): 135–49.

———. 1987. "The Politics of Economic Growth in the Industrial Democracies, 1974–1980: Leftist Strength or North Sea Oil?" *Journal of Politics* 49 (1): 242–56.

James, Simon. 1992. *British Cabinet Government*. New York: Routledge.

Jelen, Ted G., Sue Thomas, and Clyde Wilcox. 1994. "The Gender Gap in Comparative Perspective: Gender Differences in Abstract Ideology and Concrete Issues in Western Europe." *European Journal of Political Research* 25: 171–86.

Kanter, Rosabeth Moss. 1977. "Some Effects of Proportions on Group Life: Skewed Sex Rations and Responses to Token Women." *American Journal of Sociology* 82 (5): 965–90.

Kaplan, Gisela. 1992. *Contemporary Western European Feminism*. New York: New York University Press.

Keesing's Contemporary Archives. 1968–1988. New York: Longman Group.

Keman, Hans. 1991. "Ministers and Ministries." In Blondel and Thiebault 1991, 99–118.

King, A. 1981. "What Do Elections Decide?" In *Democracy at the Polls*, ed. D. Butler, H. R. Penniman, and A. Ranney. Washington DC: AEI.

Kirkpatrick, Jeane. 1974. *Political Woman*. New York: Basic Books.

Kohn, Walter S. 1980. *Women in National Legislatures: A Comparative Study of Six Countries*. New York: Praeger.

Kolinskyu, Eva. 1988. "The West German Greens—A Women's Party?" *Parliamentary Affairs* 41 (1): 129–48.

———. 1991. "Political Participation and Parliamentary Careers: Women's Quotas in West Germany." *West European Politics* 14 (1): 56–72.

———. 1992. "Women in German Political Parties and Parliaments." Paper presented at the annual meeting of the American Political Science Association, Chicago.

———. 1993. "Party Change and Women's Representation in United Germany." In Lovenduski and Norris 1993, 113–46.

Lange, Peter, and Geoffrey Garrett. 1985. "The Politics of Growth: Strategic Interaction and Economic Performance in the Advanced Industrial Democracies, 1974–1980." *Journal of Politics* 47: 792–827.

———. 1987. "The Politics of Growth Reconsidered." *Journal of Politics* 49: 257–74.

Larsson, Torbjörn. 1988. "Sweden: The New Constitution—An Old Practice Adjusted." In Blondel and Müller-Rommel 1988. 197–211.

Laver, Michael, and Norman Schofield. 1990. *Multiparty Government: The Politics of Coalition in Europe*. New York: Oxford University Press.

Leijenaar, M. H. 1991. "Participation of Women in Decision Making Bodies: The Case of the Netherlands." Unpublished paper.

———. 1993. "A Battle for Power: Selecting Candidates in the Netherlands." In Lovenduski and Norris 1993, 205–30.

Lijphart, Arend. 1968. "Typologies of Democratic Systems." *Comparative Political Studies* 1 (April): 3–44.

———. 1977. *Democracy in Plural Societies*. New Haven: Yale University Press.

———. 1984a. *Democracies: Patterns of Majoritarianism and Consensus: Government in Twenty-one Countries*. New Haven: Yale University Press.

————. 1984b. "Measures of Cabinet Durability: A Conceptual and Empirical Evaluation." *Comparative Political Studies* 17 (2): 265–79.

————. 1987. "Introduction: The Belgian Example of Cultural Coexistence in Comparative Perspective." In *Conflict and Coexistence in Belgium: The Dynamics of a Culturally Divided Society*, ed. A. Lijphart. Berkeley: University of California Press.

Ling, Yuriko, and Azusa Matsuno, with Jill M. Bystydzienski. 1992. "Women's Struggles for Empowerment in Japan." In Bystydzienski 1992b, 51–66.

Lovenduski, Joni. 1986. *Women and European Politics: Contemporary Feminism and Public Policy*. Brighton, U.K.: Harvester.

————. 1993. "Introduction: The Dynamics of Gender and Party." In Lovenduski and Norris 1993, 1–15.

Lovenduski, Joni, and Pippa Norris, eds. 1993. *Gender and Party Politics*. London: Sage.

Lovenduski, Joni, and Vicky Randall. 1993. *Contemporary Feminist Politics: Women and Power in Britain*. New York: Oxford University Press.

Low, Sidney. 1989. "The House of Commons and the Executive." In Marshall 1989b, 20–22.

MacDonald, Stuart Elaine. 1989. "A Dynamic Analysis of Parliamentary Careers." Paper presented to the Southern Political Science Association, Memphis TN.

Majendie, Paul. 1986. Reuters News Serivce. 30 December.

Mandel, Ruth. 1988. "The Political Women." In *The American Woman*, ed. Sara E. Rix. New York: W. W. Norton.

Mansbridge, Jane. 1986. *Why We Lost the ERA*. Chicago: University of Chicago Press.

Marshall, Geoffrey. 1989a. "Introduction." In Marshall 1989b, 1–16.

Marshall, Geoffrey, ed. 1989b. *Ministerial Responsibility*. New York: Oxford University Press.

Martin, Janet M. 1989. "The Recruitment of Women into Cabinets." *Western Political Quarterly* 42 (1): 161–72.

————. 1991. "An Examination of Executive Branch Appointments in the Reagan Administration by Background and Gender," *Western Political Quarterly* 44 (1): 173–84.

Matland, Richard E. 1994a. "How the Election System Structure Has Helped Women Close the Representation Gap." In *Closing the Gap: Women in Nordic Politics*, ed. Lauri Karvonen and Per Selle. Aldershot, U.K.: Dartmouth.

————. 1994b. "Institutional Variables Affecting Female Representation in National Legislatures: The Case of Norway." *Journal of Politics* 55 (3): 737–55.

————. 1994c. "Putting Scandinavian Equality to the Test: An Experimental Evaluation of Gender Stereotyping of Political Candidates in a Sample of Norwegian Voters." *British Journal of Political Science* 24 (2): 273–92.

Matland, Richard E., and Donley T. Studlar. In press. "The Contagion of Women Candidates in Single-Member District and Proportional Representation Systems: Canada and Norway." *Journal of Politics*.

McAllister, I., and D. S. Studlar. 1992. "Gender and Representation among Legislative Candidates in Australia." *Comparative Political Studies* 25: 388–411.

McDonagh, Eileen Lorenzi. 1982. "To Work or Not to Work: The Differential Impact of Achieved and Derived Status upon the Political Participation of Women, 1956–1976." *American Journal of Political Science* 26 (May): 280–97.

McHale, Vincent E., ed. 1983. *Political Parties of Europe*. Westport CT: Greenwood.

McRae, Susan. 1990. "Women at the Top: The Case of British National Politics." *Parliamentary Affairs* 43 (3): 341–47.

Means, Ingunn Norderval. 1972. "Political Recruitment of Women in Norway." *Western Political Quarterly* 5: 491–521.

Mezey, Susan Gluck. 1994. "Increasing the Number of Women in Office, Does It Matter?" In *The Year of the Woman: Myths and Realities*, ed. Elizabeth Adell Cook, Sue Thomas, and Cylde Wilcox. Boulder CO: Westview.

Michels, Robert. 1959. *Political Parties: A Sociological Study of the Oligarchical Tendencies of Modern Democracy*. New York: Dover.

Mill, John Stuart. 1970. "The Subjection of Women." In *Essays on Sex Equality*, ed. Alice S. Rossi. Chicago: University of Chicago Press.

Miller, Marjorie. 1994. "Kohl's Party Sets Quotas for Women." *Los Angeles Times*, 29 November, A4.

Mohr, Lawrence B. 1982. *Explaining Organizational Behavior*. San Francisco: Jossey-Bass.

Moncrief, Gary G., and Joel A. Thompson. 1992. "Electoral Structure and State Legislative Representation: A Research Note." *Journal of Politics* 54: 246–56.

Morley, Lord. 1989. "The Principles of Cabinet Government." In Marshall 1989b, 17–19.

Mosca, Gaetano. 1939. *The Ruling Class*. Ed. Arthur Livingston; trans. Hannah D. Kahn. Rev. ed. New York: McGraw-Hill.

Müller-Rommel, Ferdinand. 1988. "Federal Republic of Germany: A Chancellor System of Government." In Blondel and Müller-Rommel 1988, 151–66.

Norderval, Ingunn. 1985. "Party and Legislative Participation among Scandinavian Women." *Western European Politics* 8 (4): 71–89.

Norris, Pippa. 1985a. "The Gender Gap in Britain and America." *Parliamentary Affairs* 32: 192–201.

———. 1985b. "Women's Legislative Participation in Western Europe." *West European Politics* 8: 90–91.

———. 1987. *Politics and Sexual Equality: The Comparative Position of Women in Western Democracies*. Boulder CO: L. Rienner.

————. 1988. "The Gender Gap in Britain and America: A Cross-National Trend?" In *The Politics of the Gender Gap: The Social Construction of Political Influence*, ed. Carol M. Mueller. Newbury Park CA: Sage.

————. 1993. "Conclusions: Comparing Legislative Recruitment." In Lovenduski and Norris 1993, 309–30.

Norris, Pippa, and Joni Lovenduski. 1989. "Women Candidates for Parliament: Transforming the Agenda?" *British Journal of Political Science* 19: 106–15.

————. 1992. "If Only More Candidates Came Forward . . . Supply-Side Explanations of Political Representation in Britain." Paper presented at the annual meeting of the American Political Science Association, Chicago.

————. 1993. "Gender and Party Politics in Britain." In Lovenduski and Norris 1993, 35–59.

Northcutt, Wayne, and Jeffra Flaitz. 1985. "Women, Politics and the French Socialist Government." *West European Politics* 8 (4): 50–70.

Norton, Philip. 1989. "Government Defeats in the House of Commons: Myth and Reality." In Marshall 1989b, 33–45.

Nousianinen, Jaakko. 1988. "Finland." In Blondel and Müller-Rommel 1988, 213–33.

Nowotny, Helga. 1981. "Women in Public Life in Austria." In *Access to Power: Cross National Studies of Women and Elites*, ed. Cynthia Funchs Epstein and Rose Laub Coser. London: George Allen and Unwin.

Nuss, Shirley. 1985. "Women in Political Life: Variations at the Global Level." *Women and Politics* 5 (summer-fall): 65–78.

Olson, Mancur. 1971. *The Logic of Collective Action: Public Goods and the Theory of Groups*. Cambridge: Harvard University Press.

Pareto, Vilfredo. 1966. *Vilfredo Pareto: Sociological Writings*. Ed. S. E. Finer; trans. Derik Mirfin. New York: Praeger.

Pitkin, Hanna Fenichel. 1967. *The Concept of Representation*. Berkeley: University of California Press.

Przeworski, Adam, and Henry Teune. 1970. *The Logic of Comparative Social Inquiry*. New York: Wiley and Sons.

Putnam, Robert D. 1976. *The Comparative Study of Political Elites*. Englewood Cliffs NJ: Prentice-Hall.

Quindlen, Anna. 1993. "The Cement Floor." In *Thinking Out Loud: On the Personal, the Political, the Public, and the Private*, 261–63. New York: Fawcett Columbine.

Randall, Vicky. 1987. *Women and Politics: An International Perspective*. New York: St. Martin's.

Ranney, Austin. 1965. *Pathways to Parliament: Candidate Selection in Britain*. Madison: University of Wisconsin Press.

Rapoport, Ronald B. 1982. "Sex Differences in Attitude and Expression: A Generational Explanation." *Public Opinion Quarterly* 43: 18–35.

Rapoport, Ronald B., Walter Stone, and Alan I. Abramowitz. 1990. "Sex and the Caucus Participant: The Gender Gap and Presidential Nominations." *American Journal of Political Science* 34 (August): 725–40.

Rasmussen, Jorgen. 1981. "Female Career Patterns and Leadership Disabilities in Britain: The Crucial Role of Gatekeepers in Regulating Entry to the Political Elite." *Polity* 13: 600–20.

———. 1983. "The Electoral Costs of Being a Woman in the 1979 British General Election." *Comparative Politics* 15 (July): 461–75.

———. 1984. "Women in Labour: The Flapper Vote and Party System Transformation in Britain." *Electoral Studies* 3: 47–63.

Reingold, Beth. 1991. "Concepts of Representation among Female and Male State Legislators." Paper presented at the annual meeting of the American Political Science Association, Washington DC.

Reskin, Barbara. 1988. "Bringing Men Back In: Sex Differentiation and the Devaluation of Women's Work." *Gender and Society* 2: 58–81.

Riker, William. 1962. *The Theory of Political Coalitions.* New Haven: Yale University Press.

Robertson, John D. 1984. "Economic Performance and Transient European Cabinet Administrations: Implications for Consociational Parliamentary Democracies." *International Studies Quarterly* 28: 447–66.

Rohrschneider, Robert. 1994. "How Iron Is the Iron Law of Oligarchy?" *European Journal of Political Research* 25: 207–38.

Rose, Richard. 1971. "The Making of Cabinet Ministers." *British Journal of Political Science* 1: 393–414.

———. 1975. "The Making of Cabinet Ministers." In *Cabinet Studies: A Reader*, ed. Valentine Herman and James E. Alt. New York: St. Martin's.

———. 1984. *Do Parties Make a Difference?* 2nd ed. London: MacMillan.

———. 1987. *Ministers and Ministries: A Functional Analysis.* New York: Oxford University Press.

———. 1988. "Presidents and Prime Ministers." *Society* 25 (3): 61–67.

———. 1989. *The Politics of England.* 5th ed. Boston: Little Brown.

Rule, Wilma. 1981. "Why Don't Women Run: The Critical Contextual Factors in Women's Legislative Recruitment." *Western Political Quarterly* 34 (1): 60–77.

———. 1986. "Electoral Systems, Contextual Factors and Women's Opportunity for Election to Parliament in Twenty-three Democracies." *Western Political Quarterly* 40: 476–98.

———. 1989. "Why More Women Are State Legislators." *Western Political Quarterly* 43: 437–48.

Sainsbury, Diane. 1993. "The Politics of Increased Women's Representation: The Swedish Case." In Lovenduski and Norris 1993, 263–90.

Saint-Germain, Michelle A. 1989. "Does Their Difference Make a Difference? The Impact of Women on Public Policy in the Arizona Legislature." *Social Science Quarterly* 70 (4): 956–67.

Sapiro, Virginia. 1981. "Research Frontier Essay: When Are Interests Interesting? The Problem of Political Representation of Women." *American Political Science Review* 75: 701–16.

Sawer, Marian. 1990. *Sisters in Suits: Women and Public Policy in Australia.* Sydney, Australia: Allen and Unwin.

Sayrs, Lois W. 1989. *Pooled Time Series Analysis.* Newbury Park CA: Sage.

Searing, Donald. 1994. *Westminster's World: Understanding Political Roles.* Cambridge: Harvard University Press.

Sinkkonen, Sirkka, and Elina Haavio-Mannila. 1981. "The Impact of the Women's Movement and the Legislative Activity of Women MPs on Social Development." In *Women, Power and Political Systems,* ed. Margherita Rendel. London: Croom Helm.

Skard, Torild, and Elina Haavio-Mannila. 1985a. "Mobilization of Women at Elections." In Haavio-Mannila et al. 1985, 37–50.

———. 1985b. "Women in Parliament." In Haavio-Mannila et al. 1985, 51–80.

Skjeie, Hege. 1991. "The Uneven Advance of Norwegian Women." *New Left Review* 187: 79–102.

———. 1993. "Ending the Male Political Hegemony: The Norwegian Experience." In Lovenduski and Norris 1993, 231–62.

Skrede, Kari. 1990. "From Access to Integration: Women as Agents of Change in the Decision-Making Process of Public Policy." In *Women's Interests, Public Policy, and Gender Politics,* ed. Kari Skrede and Hege Skjeie. New York: UNESCO.

Smeal, Eleanor. 1984. *Why and How Women Will Elect the Next President.* New York: Harper.

Spangler, Eve, Marsha Gordon, and Ronald Pipkin. 1978. "Token Women: An Empirical Test of Kanter's Hypothesis." *American Journal of Sociology* 84: 160–70.

Studlar, Donley R., and Richard E. Matland. In press. "The Dynamics of Women's Representation in the Canadian Provinces: 1975–1994." *Comparative Journal of Political Research.*

———. 1994. "Representation of Women in the Canadian Provinces: A Preliminary Analysis." Paper presented at the Midwest Political Science Association, Chicago.

Studlar, Donley T., and Susan Welch. 1987. "Understanding the Iron Law of Andrarchy: Effects of Candidate Gender on Voting in Scotland." *Comparative Political Studies* 20: 174–91.

———. 1992. "The Party System and the Representation of Women in English Metropolitan Boroughs." *Electoral Studies* 11 (2): 62–69.

Suleiman, Ezra, ed. 1984. *Bureaucrats and Policy Making.* New York: Holmes and Meier.

Thatcher, Margaret. 1995. *The Path to Power*. New York: Harper Collins.

Theakston, Kevin. 1987. *Junior Ministers in British Government*. New York: Basil Blackwell.

Thiebault, Jean-Louis. 1988. "France." In Blondel and Müller-Rommel 1988, 86–101.

———. 1991. "The Social Background of West European Cabinet Ministers." In Blondel and Thiebault 1991, 19–30.

Thomas, Sue. 1994. *How Women Legislate*. New York: Oxford University Press.

Togeby, Lise. 1994. "Political Implicatons of Increasing Numbers of Women in the Labor Force." *Comparative Political Studies*. 27 (2): 211–40.

UNESCO. 1989. "Education at the Third Level by Type of Institution." In *Statistical Yearbook*, 3-256 to 3-262. Paris: UNESCO.

Vallance, Elizabeth. 1979. *Women in the House*. London: Athlone.

Verba, S., N. H. Nie, and J. Kim. 1978. *Political Participation and Political Equality: A Seven Nation Comparison*. Cambridge: Cambridge University Press.

Welch, Susan. 1978. "Recruitment of Women to Public Office: A Discriminant Analysis." *Western Political Quarterly* 31: 372–80.

Welch, Susan, and Donley Studlar. 1986. "British Public Opinion toward Women in Politics: A Comparative Perspective." *Western Political Quarterly* 39: 138–54.

———. 1988. "The Effects of Candidate Gender on Voting for Local Office in England." *British Journal of Political Science* 18: 273–86.

Welch, Susan, and Sue Thomas. 1988. "Explaining the Gender Gap in British Public Opinion." *Women and Politics* 8: 25–44.

Weller, Patrick. 1985. "The Vulnerability of Prime Ministers: A Comparative Perspective." *Parliamentary Affairs*, 36 (1): 96–117.

———. 1987. *First among Equals: Prime Ministers in Westminster Systems*. Boston: George Allen and Unwin.

Whip, R. 1991. "Representing Women: Australian Female Parliamentarians on the Horns of a Dilemma." *Women and Politics* 11: 1–22.

Wilcox, Clyde. 1991. "Support for Gender Equality in West Europe: A Longitudinal Analysis." *European Journal of Political Research* 20: 127–47.

———. 1994. "Why Was 1992 the 'Year of the Woman'? Explaining Women's Gains in 1992. In *The Year of the Woman: Myths and Realities*, ed. Sue Thomas, and Clyde Wilcox. Boulder CO: Westview.

Willis, Virginia. 1991. "Public Life: Women Make a Difference." Paper presented at the Expert Group Meeting's Preparations for the Interregional Consultation of the United Nations Commission on the Status of Women, May, Vienna.

Wilson, F. M. G. 1959. "The Routes of Entry of New Members of the British Cabinet." *Political Studies* 7: 222–32.

———. 1970. "Entry to the Cabinet, 1959–1968." *Political Studies* 18: 236–38.

Wilson, Harold. 1976. *The Governance of Britain*. London: Weidenfeld and Nicolson.

Wistrand, Brigita. 1981. *Swedish Women on the Move*. Ed. and trans. J. Rosen. Stockholm: Swedish Institute.

Witt, Linda, Karen M. Paget, and Glenna Matthews. 1994. *Running as a Woman: Gender and Power in American Politics*. New York: Free Press.

Wolchik, Sharon L. 1981. "Ideology and Equality: The Status of Women in Eastern and Western Europe." *Comparative Political Studies* 13 (January): 445–76.

Woldendorp, Jaap, Hans Keman, and Ian Budge. 1993. "Party Government in Twenty Democracies." *European Journal of Political Research* 24 (1): 1–119.

Yoder, Janice D. 1991. "Rethinking Tokenism: Looking Beyond Numbers." *Gender and Society* 5 (2): 178–92.

Young, Lisa. 1991. "Legislative Turnover and the Election of Women to the Canadian House of Commons." In *Women in Canadian Politics: Toward Equity in Representation*, ed. Kathy Megyery. Vol. 6. Toronto: Dundurn.

Index

collective responsibility, 11
Communist Party (Finland), 25
Conservative Party (Canada), 58
Conservative Party (U.K.), 36, 57, 59, 114
Considine, Mark, 111
consociationalism, 39–40, 113
contagion effect, 64, 89
corporatism, 109
Cotta, Maurizio, 9, 34
Cox, D. R., 78
Cresson, Edith, 1, 19, 81
critical mass, 9, 26, 64, 70–71, 89, 91, 109
Crosland, Tony, 39
Cross, J. A., 73, 75, 76
cumul des mandats, 78

Dahlerup, Drude, 18, 48, 64, 70–71, 109, 111
Dalton, Russell, 7, 108
Darcy, Robert, 2, 8, 26, 29, 33, 36, 58, 62, 77, 84
Davis, Rebecca H., 81, 86, 112, 115, 117
DeBeauvoir, Simone, 57
defense committee participation, 17, 18, 44, 49, 52–53
Demaris, Alfred, 116
Democratic Party (U.S.), 109, 115
Denmark, 3, 5, 14, 17, 33, 46, 47, 49, 51, 53, 108, 112, 114
deputy prime minister, 111
descriptive representation, 20–27, 72, 84
d'Estaing, Giscard, 21
Deutchman, Iva Ellen, 111
De Valera, Eamon, 109
de Winter, Lieven 2, 34, 38, 39, 44, 113
Diamond, Irene, 22, 23
discrimination, 67–68
Dodson, Debra, 24
Dogan, Mattei, 10, 11, 12, 13, 28, 38, 41, 42, 110
Duverger, Maurice, 7, 56
Dye, T., 58

Eduards, Maud, 5, 6, 48
education, 23, 31–34
efficacy, 24

Einhorn, Barbara, 57
Eliot, George, 72
elite theory, 30
Enloe, Cynthia, 20
Erickson, Lynda, 48
European Consortium, 60
European Free Trade Association, 5
European Parliament, 2
European Union, 5
Evans, Richard, 57

Faludi, Susan, 34, 86
family status, 22
Farrell, Brian, 42, 109
fascism, 4
Feinstein, Dianne, 21
feminism, 34, 57, 108
Finland, 5, 12, 13, 14, 25, 30, 40, 46, 47, 49, 64–65, 81
Finnish Communist Party, 25
Flaitz, Jeffra, 47
Flammang, Janet, 19
Foot, Michael, 39
Fraktionen (FRG), 111
France, 3, 12, 14, 16, 21, 30, 46, 49, 56, 78, 81, 107, 108, 109, 112
Free Democratic Party (FRG), 23
Frognier, Andre Paul, 30, 56, 111

Gaitskell, Hugh, 39
Gallagher, Michael, 11, 45, 107
Galligan, Yvonne, 7, 11
Gandhi, Indira, 20, 21, 27
Garrett, Geoffrey, 58
Gelb, Joyce, 5, 20, 25, 26, 108, 112
gender gap, 7, 108, 112
generalist, 8, 38
Gerlich, Peter, 38, 40
Germany, 3, 6, 7, 14, 17, 23, 46, 49, 57, 108, 109, 111
Giroud, Francoise, 21
Graves, Pamela, 57
Greece, 4, 21, 57, 82, 88, 113
Greens (FRG), 7, 23, 59
Guadagnini, Marila, 7

Haavio-Mannila, Elina, 18, 33, 48, 56, 59
Halsaa, Beatrice, 5, 47

Hanninen-Salmelin, Evan, 48
Hansen, Preben, 3
Heath, Edward, 82, 83, 107
Hernes, Helga Marie, 48, 59
Hills, J., 22
Hornsby-Smith, Pat, 82
House of Commons (U.K.), 22, 30, 39, 41, 45

Iceland, 4, 5
ideology, 9, 56, 58, 65–66, 70, 71
incumbency, 77, 78, 79, 80, 81, 83, 85, 116
individual responsibility, 11
Inglehart, Ronald, 7, 47, 108
inner cabinets, 13, 16
institutional culture, 71, 111
Inter-Parliamentary Union, 17, 60, 115
Ireland, 15, 42, 46, 49, 108, 109, 113
iron law of andrarchy, 10, 30
Italy, 1, 3, 4, 19, 42, 46, 49, 53, 108

Jackman, Robert, 58
James, Simon, 11, 12, 109
Jelen, Ted G., 7, 108
junior ministers, 13, 40–41, 42, 107, 110

Kanawa, Kiri Te, 83
Kanter, Rosabeth Moss, 18, 19, 24, 53, 54, 111, 117
Kaplan, Gisela, 3, 4, 5, 6, 21, 25, 31, 33, 34, 47, 56, 57, 78, 108, 112, 114
Keman, Hans, 56, 60, 107
Kim, J., 33
King, A., 58
Kohl, Helmut, 7
Kohn, Walter S., 36
Kolinsky, Eva, 7, 22, 23, 59
Kwenna Listin, 4

Labor Party (Norway), 89
Labour Party (U.K.), 7, 36, 57, 58, 78, 114, 115
Lancaster, Thomas D., 81, 86, 115
Lange, Peter, 58
Larsson, Torbjorn, 40, 42, 87
Laver, Michael, 2, 107
"law of increasing disproportions," 28, 30

Leijenaar, M. H., 7, 18
Liberal Party (U.K.), 59, 70
Lijphart, Arend, 13, 40, 113
Lovenduski, Joni, 1, 3, 4, 6, 7, 16, 19, 20, 25, 26, 42, 43, 48, 56, 57, 58, 59, 65, 70, 78, 80, 82, 88, 108, 115
Luxembourg, 5
Luxemburg, Rosa, 4

MacDonald, Stuart Elaine, 2, 36, 43, 68, 114
Macmillan, Harold, 19
Mair, Peter, 60
Majendie, Paul, 35
Major, John, 7, 45, 82
Mandel, Ruth, 27
Marshall, Geoffrey, 20
Martin, Janet M., 7, 72, 73, 74, 77, 79, 86, 107, 110
Matland, Richard E., 7, 26, 28, 33, 48, 58, 62, 64, 77, 83, 114
Matthews, Glenna, 20, 27, 111, 112
Mauroy, Pierre, 16
Mazur, Amy, 7
McHale, Vince E., 60
Means, Ingunn Norderval, 10
media, 74, 77, 79, 80, 85, 86, 117
Meir, Golda, 20
Michels, Robert, 30
Mikulski, Barbara, 27
Mill, John Stuart, 10
Miller, Marjorie, 7
Mitterrand, Francois, 56, 114
Mohr, Lawrence B., 64
Moncrief, Gary G., 84
Morgan, Elystan, 41
Mosca, Gaetano, 30
Müller, Wolfgang C., 38, 40
Müller-Rommel, Ferdinand, 2, 13, 16, 110
Mussolini, Benito, 4
Myrdal, Alva, 3

National Socialism, 4
The Netherlands, 3, 6, 11, 14, 16, 17, 21, 39–40, 44, 45, 46, 49, 81, 108, 113
New Politics, 108
Nie, N. H., 33
Nordboe, Eldrid, 81

Norris, Pippa, 1, 2, 6, 7, 25, 33, 47, 56, 57, 58, 62, 65, 88, 90, 108, 114, 115
Northcutt, Wayne, 47
Norway, 1, 5, 10, 14, 15, 16, 24, 27, 28, 29, 31, 32, 46, 47, 48, 49, 81, 82, 86, 89, 112, 114
Norwegian Labor Party, 29
Nousiainen, Jaakko, 12, 13, 40, 42, 56
Nowotny, Helga, 112

Oeyangen, Gunhild, 81
Official Governments Secrets Act (U.K.), 42
organization theory, 53, 64

Paget, Karen M., 20, 27, 111, 112, 117
Pareto, Vilfredo, 30
parliamentary committees, 17
party competition, 64, 88
party discipline, 25, 26
party size, 64, 66
Petersen, Oddrun, 81
Pintasilgo, Dr. Maria de Lurdes, 19, 21
Pintat, Christina, 115
Pitkin, Hanna Fenichel, 1
political culture, 8, 15, 47–49, 51–52, 54, 66–67, 87, 114
pool of eligibles, 8, 29, 90
portfolios, 8, 16, 56, 81, 85, 107, 110
Portugal, 4, 14, 21, 31, 32, 112, 113
positive action, 36, 51, 67–68
positive discrimination, 36, 51, 67–68, 89
preferential voting, 48, 114
Prime Ministers, 19–20, 73, 75
Putnam, Robert D., 2, 10, 20, 28, 30

Quindlen, Anna, 29

Randall, Vicky, 3, 4, 6, 7, 22, 33, 43, 59, 70, 78, 108
Ranney, Austin, 30, 59
Rantzen, Esther, 83
Rapoport, Ronald B., 24
recruitment norms, 8, 66–67, 86, 90, 117
Redstockings (Iceland), 4
Rehn, Elizabeth, 81
Reingold, Beth, 24, 111

Republic of Ireland, 44
reshuffles, 73, 75, 83, 85
Reskin, Barbara, 111
Reuters, 116
Richards, Ann, 20, 21, 111
Riker, William, 2
Riksdag, 25
Rimington, Stella, 83
Robinson, Mary, 1
Rohrschneider, Robert, 8
Rose, Richard, 3, 9, 10, 11, 12, 13, 34, 41, 42, 57, 58, 73, 74, 81, 107, 108, 110, 115
Rule, Wilma, 2, 47, 84, 115

"sacrificial lambs," 57
Sainsbury, Diane, 7
Saint-Germain, Michelle A., 19, 26
Salazar, Antonio, 31, 112
Sawer, Marian, 25, 26
Scandinavia, 3, 14, 28, 33, 34, 47–49, 51–52, 57, 66, 109, 114
"Scandinavian Myth," 48
Schofield, Norman, 2, 107
Searing, Donald, 10, 30, 39, 41, 43, 113
second wave of the feminist movement, 3, 5–7, 27, 58, 108
sectorization, 16, 17, 18, 88
Sinn Féin, 35, 109
Skard, Torild, 18, 24, 33, 43, 48, 56, 59
Skjeie, Hege, 5, 7, 48
Skrede, Kari, 10
Smeal, Eleanor, 25, 111
Snell, E. J., 78
Social Democratic Party (Finland), 65
Social Democratic Party (FRG), 23
Social Democrats (U.K.), 70
Socialists (Greece), 57
Spain, 4, 6, 13, 15, 32, 113
specialist, 8, 38
Storting (Norway), 24
Studlar, Donley, 28, 33, 48, 57, 58, 64, 73, 77
Supreme Court (U.S.), 72
Sweden, 1, 3, 5, 14, 25, 32, 33, 40, 45, 46, 47, 49, 86, 108, 110, 113
Switzerland, 5, 108

Taylor, Charles, 41

In the Women and Politics series

Volume 1
Women, Elections, and Representation, 2nd ed.,
revised by R. Darcy, Susan Welch, and Janet Clark

Volume 2
Women and Power in Parliamentary Democracies:
Cabinet Appointments in Western Europe, 1968–1992
By Rebecca Howard Davis